Mike is a masterful storyteller. As I read his new book, *Potevka's Gifts*, it was as if I was right there with him experiencing his pain and joy. There are few books out there that can fill the soul with a sense of thankfulness and gratitude for all we have; Mike's book does that and more. Mike recently came to our town to speak; 1300 people were in attendance. His patriotic messages strike a chord with people of all ages.

—Ryan Montgomery

What a great read! Mr. Ramsdell answered many of my "I wonder" questions from reading *A Train to Potevka*. His enthusiasm and love of God and country definitely come through in these anecdotes. There are some wonderfully thought-provoking moments in this book, especially concerning the events and aftermath of 9/11.

—Annette Boren

This is a book you will be compelled to read in one sitting. This collection of stories is spell binding. I read it twice in one sitting. The story about the wolf is marvelous.

—Rick Stevens

PRAISE FOR MIKE'S MESSAGE

"Brother Ramsdell, your recent presentation to our Brigham Young Emeriti Alumni Association, was truly a spiritual feast as well as a spell-binding story of your personal experiences. The BYU facility near Sundance was completely sold out for your keynote address and beautiful uplifting message. It was all we could have hoped for and more."

—Stanley Peterson, President BYU
Emeriti Alumni Association

Mike Ramsdell is one of a kind; an American original. One of the most fascinating men I have had the pleasure to meet . . . Working with Mike to make *A Train to Potevka* a screenplay and production as a major motion picture has been a pure pleasure. He is a positive, patriotic, people person and *Potevka* is a story that goes beyond adventure and changes lives.

—Kieth Merrill, Writer and Producer
Academy Award-Winning Director

"Mike, thank you for speaking at the Twenty-First Annual Conference for Seniors. We were pleased that it turned out to be a terrific success! As you may know, we had approximately 1,000 conference attendees. Once again, thank you for taking the time to come and make this year's conference the success it was."

—Orrin G. Hatch
United States Senator

POTEVKA'S GIFTS

by

Mike Ramsdell

To

Ned,

Enjoy!   Mike

Всего Хорошего
(all the best)
Mike Ramsdell

POTEVKA'S GIFTS

Copyright 2012 © by Michael A. Ramsdell

Library of Congress Catalog Card Number – Pending

Second Printing

ISBN 978-9832034-1-4

Personalized books and e-books can be ordered at
www.michaelramsdell.com

Please send correspondence to:
Zhivago Press
P.O. BOX 1792
Layton, UT 84041-6792

or by email to:
mikeramsdell1776@gmail.com

For speaking engagements or cruise lecture schedules
please call (801) 444-1776 or go to
www.michaelramsdell.com

Printed in the USA

DEDICATION

Bon,
You were there during the lean and mean of Russia. You have been at my side ever since. And what an incredible ride it has been!

Mike

Grow old along with me!
The best is yet to be,
The last of life for which the first was made.

                                    R. Browning

Table of Contents

PREFACE

Dear Reader,

First, let me say how grateful I am to you for helping to make my first book, *A Train to Potevka*, a national best seller. I am honored at the response from so many people. Over the last few years, hundreds of thousands of readers have embraced the book and its message of family, patriotism, and love of country. I have received cards, letters, and emails from across the United States and, even, from other countries thanking me for writing the book. I am humbled that my story has somehow touched so many people in a positive way.

From its meager first printing five years ago of only 100 books, we estimate that a million-plus people have now read *Potevka*. This figure represents our Zhivago Press sales, Costco sales, national and local bookstore sales, the library system, and the passing of the book from one person to another to another to another.

Some ask, why then, has *Potevka* not appeared on the *New York Times* Best Sellers list? The answer has to do with the fact that a huge portion of our book sales have come from Costco which does not report its sales to outside sources or to national book listings. Had that not been the case, *A Train to Potevka* would have been on the *New York Times* Best Sellers list three years ago.

Keeping in mind the old adage of "*Never judge a book by its cover*," please don't judge this book by its cover or its title. This book, *Potevka's Gifts*, is not the promised sequel to *A Train to Potevka*. It is not a spy thriller, and it is not a novel. It is a collection of stories—a memoir—written as if you and I were together at a local café having an informal conversation as best friends.

The book is written in two halves: the first is about experiences and people who have had a profound and lasting effect on my life. The second half, which could be considered more fun and lighthearted, was especially written for the readers and audience members who have read the book or heard me speak and want to have the answers to the most-often-asked questions about *Potevka* and my career all in one place. Some of the anecdotes have nothing to do with the original book or my career; however, most of them are ones I often share with audiences during my speaking events.

Why the title *Potevka's Gifts* for this book? Because of just that . . . gifts. *A Train to Potevka* has brought so many blessings and "gifts" into my life

And, why? Perhaps that can be answered by the following:

In my account of what could have been my final days at the safe house in Potevka, I share with the reader the promise I made to the Lord that if he would help me make it through my ordeal, I would try to become a new man—I would never take my blessings for granted, I would try to live the best possible life I could, and I would give back to others.

I certainly don't want to imply that I have reached any of those self-imposed goals, but I have tried. From the unexpected incident of fracturing my neck, which lead to writing *Potevka*, to having the opportunity to speak to hundreds of audiences from all walks of life while sharing a message of patriotism, freedom, and the concern of a loving Heavenly Father— my life *has* been blessed. Thus, considering all the good things that have happened since my years in Russia, *Potevka's Gifts* is the perfect title for this anthology.

When I wrote *A Train to Potevka*, we chose to have it classified as fiction in order to avoid any conflict my book might present. We did this because, as a former agent, I am subject to certain federal laws and regulations that govern what can and cannot be disclosed about my former work. Being restricted in what I can write is not the case with *Potevka's Gifts*. However, as a story teller, I still wanted to have "creative license" while writing an essentially non-fiction book. I wanted the characters to have dialogue, the stories to be as real as possible, and, most of all, I wanted to make each one readable and enjoyable. Therefore, a few of the events, dates, places, and names in the book have been altered or fictionalized. Also, if there are any mistakes or inaccuracies in the book, they are entirely mine.

If you have not read *A Train to Potevka*, not to worry; I believe most of these stories can be enjoyed on their own merits. For those who have already read *Potevka*, I hope you will find this collection gratifying, compelling, entertaining, and that it will bring back some fond memories.

Finally, the little boy on the front cover sitting on the sack of potatoes is me. It is one of only a few photographs taken of me as a child before I went to grade school. I was told that it was taken in the backyard of my boyhood home in Bear River. From those early years of my childhood to today . . . what a journey it has been!

I hope you enjoy the book.

Всего Хорошего
Mike Ramsdell

POTEVKA'S GIFTS

by

Mike
Ramsdell

There will come a time when you believe everything is finished. That will be the beginning.

Louis L'Amour

THE ADVENTURE
CONTINUES

THE STOCKHOLM WOLF

ICHABOD CRANE

ABDUL'S AMERICA

Chapter 1

THE
STOCKHOLM
WOLF

The wolf is at the door.
Norwegian proverb

Perhaps you can imagine the excitement Bonnie and I felt when we got word from the movie company which had purchased the film rights to my book, *A Train to Potevka,* that we were being asked to accompany them on a trip to the former Soviet Union to scout out filming locations.

Although we had signed a contract with the movie company several months earlier, the idea of actually traveling with several movie executives to explore areas where the village of

Potevka could be replicated, truly brought into focus that my book *really* was going to be made into a movie. After a few weeks, we received a packet from the film company containing our airline tickets, the trip itinerary and a roster of those who would be traveling with us.

Months before our trip, those of us involved in the project had endless conversations regarding the advantages and disadvantages of filming on location in Russia. We were warned by other Hollywood film studios of the difficulties and perils of filming in the former USSR because of the problems we could encounter with the mafia. Arguably, since the fall of the Soviet Empire in the early '90s, the Russian mafia has controlled most of the country: the businesses, the banks, the police, the politicians. Their influence was, and still is, everywhere.

When attempting any kind of business transaction in Russia, foreign or domestic, it is understood at the outset that a 30% fee must be paid to the Russian mafia. The mafia refers to this 30% as protection money—a fee to protect a new business enterprise from criminals—as if to imply the mafia are not criminal. Bottom line, this 30% protection money is out-and-out extortion.

It doesn't matter if you're a big, Huntsman-like international company or a small mom-

and-pop kiosk selling candy and Cokes, every enterprise is expected to pay this protection fee. If this extortion money is not paid, and in a timely manner, the mafia will, by whatever means, eliminate the business.

Jon Huntsman took his highly successful international company into Russia in the early 1990s with the humanitarian goal of creating a large chemical/plastics business that would provide jobs for the struggling Russian people. After only a few years of constantly fighting the corruption, bureaucracy, government, and politicians—which all had ties to the mafia— Huntsman finally had had enough. He shut down his business and pulled out of the fledgling Russian democracy to which he had simply wanted to give a helping hand.

Huntsman's experience was not unique. After the fall of the Soviet Empire, hundreds of foreign companies expanded their businesses and moved into Russia to help the economy and, no doubt, also take advantage of potential business opportunities—a win-win for Russia's new free market economy. With rare exception, the story's outcome was always the same: the American or European company, well established and very successful in other countries around the world, would be matched up with a Soviet counterpart and, as per Russian law, a mandatory joint venture would be formed. In most cases, the foreign company would provide all the capital, all the resources, all the technical know-how, all the management, and all the marketing. The Russian side of the joint venture provided nothing except to share in the profits, even though the business joint venture was to be a 50/50 contribution by both sides of the partnership.

In the end, once the new business was firmly established and monetarily successful, the foreign partner would suddenly become persona non grata, or found guilty of violating Russian tax law, or found guilty of some criminal activity, or whatever, and then be required to leave the country. The Russian joint venture partner would then take over the business totally.

Now, twenty years since the collapse of the USSR, the influence of the Russian mafia is as strong as it has ever been, if not stronger.

Thus, with this knowledge and the several warnings from others in the movie business, it was agreed from the outset that our film company would not film in Russia thereby avoiding the potential mafia problem.

The night we flew across the Atlantic, I had to pinch myself when thinking of what was about to take place. I thought of what a great experience this was going to be: flying around eastern Europe and the former USSR with a group of Hollywood movie executives, staying in lavish hotels, eating marvelous meals, and pretending to do work like the typical Hollywood stereotypes. In actuality, our work there was just the opposite of what I expected; we were busy every minute, from early morning to late at night.

We were always up early for breakfast to go over the day's schedule. Afterwards, we boarded vans or a bus and headed out to scout predetermined sites for shooting the film. All the while doing this, I had a microphone attached to the front of my jacket, as did Kieth Merrill, the film's creative director. Thus, we made an ongoing narrative at each location for review once we returned to the States. Not only were we both miked, we had a cameraman constantly with us who shot our observations and conversations at all the potential filming locations.

Somewhere along the way we would have lunch and then continue our busy scouting pace through the afternoon. My ideas about hobnobbing with the Hollywood movie types changed 180 degrees from my original thoughts. Bonnie and I were very impressed by how seriously and professionally they went about their business.

In the early evening, we would return to our hotel and have a half hour or so back in our rooms to freshen up before dinner. Sitting around the dining table, we would review the activities of the day and usually get into long discussions—sometimes heated discussions— as to new ideas or additions to the *Potevka* screenplay.

One evening, Kieth Merrill brought up a particular scene in the movie where I am in the safe house, surrounded by wolves, which is directly out of my book. Kieth, however, wanted to expand the scene by having the lead wolf of the pack smash through the window of the cabin with the intent of eating me for dinner.

"No way," I said, as every eye around the dinner table turned in my direction to see my reaction to Kieth's suggestion.

"Kieth, I grew up a country boy, a farm boy, and had dogs all my life. No wolf would behave like that. It just wouldn't happen. And wolves, as I understand, are quite docile by nature."

"But just think about it," he said. "The audience would be on the edge of their seats . . . they would love it."

At the outset of our trip, I remember Kieth admonishing all of us,

"Look, I have no corner on creativity. We want everyone's best ideas so we can make this a terrific, successful movie."

This from a man with an Academy Award, forty years in the business, and thirty-plus movies to his credit. We all appreciated Kieth's openness and attitude. Just the same, I stood my ground; a wolf would never behave in such an aggressive way. The audience just wouldn't buy it.

At the end of our debates about the wolf, Kieth would usually finish with, "Just think about it, Mike. Just give it a chance."

After our weeks of scouting several Eastern European locations, our group made the decision that Lithuania would be the best location to film our movie.

Lithuania is one of the three Baltic countries that was controlled by the Soviets during the 45 years of the Cold War. We found the country had everything we needed for our movie and, most importantly, there was little mafia there.

The capital, Vilnius, looks a great deal like parts of Moscow. On the outskirts of Vilnius we found several locations with facilities that we could use to replicate the village of Potevka, including the safe house, the train station, the old church, and the *dachas*. We also found all the old *comradskis* and *babushkas* (grandmas) we would need for the film.

Vilnius is also the headquarters of a very successful British film studio. Years earlier this studio had moved their operations from London to this Baltic capital because of all that it offered as a backdrop for making movies— particularly Russian-genre films—including the lack of mafia interference, as well as substantially lower costs for goods and services. They had done several first run movies there and were in agreement with us that we had made the right decision not to deal with the mafia and corruption in Russia.

During our last night in Vilnius, gathered around the large, oak dining table at the hotel, our group became rather nostalgic knowing that our time together was about to end. While finishing our last evening meal, Kieth couldn't resist bringing up, one last time, the idea about the scene where he wanted the alpha wolf to break through the glass window of the safe house and attack me. (Actually it would, of course, be a trained wolf, and the lead actor would be the one to engage the wolf.)

Again, I held my ground that a wolf would not behave like that. "The audience just would not buy it," I said repeatedly.

"A wolf," I told him again, "is naturally fearful of humans. Trust me, Kieth, from an old farm boy, it just wouldn't happen."

And again, Kieth's usual retort,

"Just think about it . . . give it a chance."

We agreed to address the issue again once we returned to the States and continued our work on the screenplay.

The next morning, Bon and I packed our suitcases, ate breakfast together with our group, loaded in the van and headed for the airport. Midmorning, all of the movie executives were flying to Morocco for two additional days of scouting before returning to the United States.

After hugs and goodbyes, Bonnie and I watched as their flight departed.

We had a couple of hours to wait for our own short flight from Vilnius to Helsinki, Finland, where I had maintained an apartment for the ten years I was working in and out of Russia on behalf of the State Department.

Helsinki, one of our very favorite cities in Europe, is the closest western capital to Moscow—approximately 1,000 kilometers away. While the rest of our group would be in Morocco, Bonnie and I would spend three days checking out various locations in Helsinki that might be used as part of our movie.

For the next two days, Bon and I visited the prospective sites: the downtown area, Embassy Row, the island of Lauttasaari, my old apartment building, and Malmi, located on the outskirts of the city, where our team did part of our covert training.

Knowing that once our Helsinki work was done and we would be flying back to America, Bonnie and I decided to take a day off and travel on the overnight Silja Line ship from Helsinki to Stockholm.

Stockholm, the capital of Sweden, is also one of our favorite places in Europe. We've found the Scandinavian people of the North to be absolutely wonderful: friendly, kind, and industrious. These countries of Scandinavia are a must-visit location for any traveler. During our years of living in Helsinki, Bonnie and I would take the overnight ship from Helsinki to Stockholm whenever we had a rare free weekend. As mentioned in *Potevka*, Bon and I were married in the Stockholm Temple. Therefore, this beautiful Scandinavia capital has an extra special meaning for us.

Knowing we would be in Stockholm for just one day, Bon and I decided to leave our suitcases in storage at our Helsinki hotel room. We took just a couple of small backpacks containing the bare overnight essentials of a toilet kit, camera, cell phone, passports, money, and nothing else.

The Silja Line ships that sail between Helsinki and Stockholm are some of the largest passenger ships in the world—certainly the largest in Scandinavia where, by the way, the majority of cruise ships are built. With a capacity of 3000 passengers each, the two huge Silja Line ships travel nightly between Helsinki and Stockholm. One ship leaves Helsinki each night at 5:00 PM, while the other leaves Stockholm at the same time. They actually pass one another in the Baltic Sea during the night. The journey, depending on the weather in the sea, takes fifteen hours. You can set your watch by their on-time punctuality.

Like most cruise ships, there are a number of on-board activities to enjoy—dining, shopping, dancing, swimming, sauna—the list is endless. And those who have experienced traveling on these ships can attest that the industrious, hard-working Finns and Swedes who travel on these ships definitely know how to party when it's time to play!

Bonnie and I boarded our ship an hour early at 4:00 PM. We checked in, located our room, and then took the elevators directly to the eleventh floor top deck of the ship to secure two lounge chairs near the rear of the ship. We wanted to take advantage of the panoramic views while leaving the Port of Helsinki. Being able to see close up the literally thousands of islands located in the North Sea between Finland and Sweden is an unforgettable experience.

On several similar occasions during the summer months, Bon and I have stayed up all night during the crossing because it remains light most of the night. Located so close to the North Pole, it only gets dusk for about an hour or so around two o'clock in the morning when the night sky opens up with billions of stars overhead. There truly is no place like Scandinavia in the summer: great weather, great times, and wonderful people!

Because of our demanding schedule the previous two days, Bon and I returned to our ship cabin around 2:00 AM. In the morning after the mandatory Scandinavian breakfast buffet of smoked salmon, capers, pickled herring, Karelian pies, yogurt, and fruit, we were back up on the top deck to see the charming, old-world sights as the huge ship glided into the Silja Line Port not far from downtown Stockholm. It was 9:00 AM when we arrived.

Like two kids visiting an amusement park, we were excited to be back in Stockholm. At breakfast, we had planned out the entire day. We basically had seven hours in Stockholm, from 10:00 AM to 5:00 PM, at which time we would board the ship for our return trip to Helsinki. Once we disembarked, we headed directly to one of our favorite places to visit— the Vasa Museum.

Back in the early 1600s, the Vasa was to be the crown jewel of the powerful Swedish Navy. Its construction was the pride and joy of their military and the pet project of the Swedish King. No expense was spared in equipping and decorating this beautiful, state-of-the-art ship. It was designed by the best ship builders and craftsmen of the time.

Built for speed, at only 120 feet in length and heavily armed with 64 cannons and guns, the Vasa began her maiden voyage out of Stockholm on August 10, 1628. Several hundred yards out into the bay, the ship suddenly keeled over and sank, taking fifty men to their watery graves.

For 330 years the Vasa lay at the bottom of the sea. A salvage and restoration project began in 1961. Today, the ship is a major tourist attraction in Stockholm. It is now housed in a museum close to downtown. If you—and I hope you do—ever travel to Stockholm, the Vasa is a must-see.

After the Vasa, we visited the nearby Galärparken. This park has acres and acres of walking and bike paths, dozens of small lakes for boating and recreation, and endless beautiful public gardens.

Taxes are very high in the Scandinavian countries. However, the governments wisely use a large portion of tax revenues to create and maintain beautiful public parks and venues for the general population.

Sensing the day was flying by, we next took the local water ferry to the Royal Palace, the official residence of the Swedish monarchy. It is the largest palace in Europe still in use as a residence by a royal family, with over 600 magnificent rooms, including five museums. This popular landmark is, also, a must-see for any visitor to the Swedish capital.

After lunch at a local cafeteria—delicious Scandahoovian soup and bread—we made our way to nearby Old Town located in the heart of the city. This area consists of old homes, shops, and businesses dating back to the 1600s. There is so much to see and do in the Old Town that just a few hours cannot do justice to capture its charm, beauty, and fascinating history.

While window shopping in Old Town, I noticed that it was already half-past three. I told Bon that we had better start making our way back to the Central Railway Station where we would catch a local subway train which would take us out to the Silja dock where our cruise ship was being readied for its return trip to Helsinki.

Once we arrived at the station, we saw directly across the street, much to our delight, the Promised Land . . . McDonald's! When traveling the world, and in a bind for some quick, reliable food, thankfully, there always seems to be a McDonald's not far away.

Checking our watches, we decided we had just enough time to make a quick visit. We hurried across the street, entered McDonald's, and ordered our usual fare of cheeseburgers, fries, and Cokes. Hungry from our day's activities, we "*wolfed*" down our food. (Notice, I use the word *"wolf.")* It seems I'm always hungry when traveling.

Once finished with Ronald McDonald's cuisine, we again checked the time, grabbed our backpacks and headed towards the exit. As we walked outside the McDonald's entrance, ten feet away, sitting directly in front of us, were two large dogs tied up to a railing. Both being dog and cat lovers, Bon and I paused for a moment to look at the two animals. Noticing our apparent interest, the two dogs stared directly back at us. Then Bon interrupted,

"Mike, look, that one animal is a Russian wolf."

Immediately my eyes were cast in the wolf's direction. Sadly, both dogs were tied to the railing with old, worn, hay ropes. On closer observation, the two dogs, a German Shepherd and the Russian wolf, were both visibly malnourished.

15

And while watching the wolf the entire time, what was I thinking? Of course, about our movie and Kieth Merrill's insistence regarding the confrontation with the lead wolf at the safe house which he wanted in our movie.

Never approaching the animals, after two or three minutes I told Bon that we had to go in order to make it to our ship on time.

As we turned to walk away, without any warning, the wolf that had never taken his eyes off me for the entire time I'd been watching him, suddenly leaped the ten feet from where he was sitting and attacked me. Snarling viciously, he clamped his powerful jaws around my left thigh muscle and tried violently to wrestle me to the ground.

The moment became surreal.

My first concern was how to protect Bonnie once I got the wolf off of me. She stood directly behind me, speechless, while I tried to force my hands into the wolf's mouth to pry it open. With one hand in his lower jaw, and the fingers of my other hand around his snout, slowly, I was able to pry his vice-like jaws apart. As I freed myself, the growling wolf, still never taking his eyes off of me, cautiously backed away to the railing where the upset German Shepherd sat on his haunches howling uncontrollably.

By then a large group of Swedish people had gathered around me in front of the McDonald's. There I stood, not believing what had just happened. The wolf had completely ripped my Levi's from my thigh down to my ankle. If his teeth had been a few inches in another direction, I would forever be singing with the sopranos back home in our church choir.

I stood stunned, one leg naked, my Levi's ripped apart, and the left leg of my garments in tatters. The worrisome part was that my upper thigh, where the wolf had clamped onto me, was turning multiple colors of dark purple and red, and swelling bigger and bigger by the minute.

Totally shaken, and trying to make sense of what had just happened, suddenly, an older Swedish couple came hurriedly out of McDonald's and approached me.

"Sir," they said—speaking perfect English— "we saw what just happened. When the wolf attacked you, a woman eating with her husband inside McDonald's jumped up and quickly ran out of the building. That is her," the wife said, pointing in the direction where a woman was running from McDonald's to the opposite side of the street to the train station.

Needless to say, my head was spinning.

"And sir," the lady said, "her husband or boyfriend is still in the restaurant eating."

Against Bonnie's protests, I defiantly limped into McDonald's. All eyes were on me, waiting for the confrontation. The old couple pointed out where the man was sitting while they used their cell phone to call the police.

As I approached him, the shabbily-dressed man looked up at me, as if he was not all that concerned.

"Was that your dog that attacked me?" I demanded, as I stood at his table.

"It depends which dog you are talking about," he said in broken English, as he took another bite from his hamburger.

"You know the animal I'm talking about!" I said in a raised voice. "The Russian wolf!"

And right out of a "Pink Panther" movie: "That's not my dog," he replied, not even looking at me as he continued eating.

I was so angry with his I-don't-care attitude; I hoped he would choke on one of his French fries. I asked him for his name and address in anticipation of the arrival of the police, but, of course, he refused to provide any information whatsoever.

After his continued silence and smirks to my questions, Bonnie and the old couple followed me outside, where we waited for the police to arrive. While Bonnie and the McDonald's manager attended to my wounds with disinfectant, gauze and tape from a medical kit, from time to time I glanced over at the upset, trembling dogs. Despite what had happened, I felt sorry for them, especially the wolf; he was still so agitated and his eyes followed my every move.

Ten minutes passed when suddenly the woman reappeared who earlier had run out of the restaurant. Through the glass of the entrance door, I watched as she spoke with her man still sitting inside McDonald's. Soon they grabbed their few belongings and walked together out the front door. As they untied the dogs and started to leave, I stood in front of them, blocking their exit, while they held back the dogs.

"You are not going to leave until the police arrive," I said emphatically, pointing to my wounded, ugly leg.

"You stupid American," the man answered as he maneuvered the troubled wolf in front of him, a few feet from where I was standing. "Do you want to go at this again? But this time with both dogs?" he asked.

Looking at the man and woman close up, their dress, poor physical condition, and the few belongings they were carrying, I was certain they were both drug addicts. This was later confirmed by the police who, regrettably, didn't arrive before the couple disappeared into the busy afternoon crowd at the Central Railway

Station with the Russian wolf and German Shepherd in tow.

When the police finally showed up, I had a few choice words to say about Sweden's liberal drug laws when they confirmed, from our description, that the man and woman were known drug addicts living on the streets, and surviving on government welfare.

Looking at my watch, it was doubtful if Bon and I could make it back in time to the pier to catch our ship back to Helsinki. The kind, old couple, along with the police, insisted that I get medical attention immediately. However, I knew there was a doctor and medical staff on the ship—and more importantly—Bonnie and I had airline tickets that would take us back home to America in less than 48 hours. We had to be on that ship!

Foregoing the local train, Bon and I caught a taxi that delivered us to the Silja ship just as it was ready to depart. Understandably, to other ship passengers, I'm sure it had to be a comical sight as we boarded the ship; me walking up the gangplank, limping on my one good leg, my other leg nearly naked, and my Levi's ripped almost stem to stern.

After getting to our cabin, I stripped down to see how bad the injury was. The area where the wolf had mauled me was so swollen, it seemed the surrounding skin was going to burst. Once I had made myself as presentable as possible—I had no other change of clothes—Bon and I made our way to the main administration area of the ship, to the dispensary. With only a towel covering my lower body, an attractive, blond, Swedish, female doctor—could it have been otherwise?—could not believe our story as she examined my injuries.

"I've heard of wolf attacks," she said, "but never in downtown Stockhold, especially not in front of the McDonald's across from the main train station."

Once she completed her exam, she gave us the bad news.

"Mr. Ramsdell," she said," because of your injuries and the severity of the attack, and, especially, not knowing if the wolf was rabid or not, I'm certain you are not going to be able to leave the country. You will have to stay here in Scandinavia under mandatory government quarantine for at least the next three months."

"What! There's no possible way," I whispered to Bonnie under my breath. Back home we had a movie screenplay to finish; and, in only a few months, the movie would go into pre-production. "I can't possibly be quarantined here for three months! It's not going to happen!" And what would Bon and I do for these three months?

21

After awhile I stopped, came to my senses, and began to think of the possibilities. My portion of the screenplay could actually be done by computer over the Internet. We were only an hour away by air from the neighboring country of Lithuania, where the movie would be shot. I wondered . . . *Would the Baltics be part of the quarantine?*

"And best of all," the doctor said, "under our socialized system, the government would pick up the entire bill and pay all your expenses."

Now how's that for the chance to spend a perfect summer? Bonnie, me, and wonderful Scandinavia for three months—all expenses paid!

On the way back to our cabin, we stopped in one of the clothing shops on the main floor of the ship. There I was able to purchase a pair of cargo shorts that I could wear until we got back to our luggage in Helsinki.

What a day it had been. Coming down from such an adrenaline rush, I could only think about food and drink. I needed some quick energy to keep me going.

After dinner, and before returning to our cabin for the night, we stopped by the ship's business center where I paid for an hour's time to use the Internet on one of the computers. Knowing each of the movie executives always had their Apple computers with them, I spent the hour composing a blow-by-blow email account of what had happened with the wolf at McDonald's.

I concluded the email with the following words:

> *PS: If you are ever asked to accompany a group of movie executives to the countries of Eastern Europe to do a movie scout, and if the director wants to add a scene where the lead wolf in the film smashes through the cabin window to attack the occupant—you don't argue with the director by saying:*
>
> *"That would never happen! The movie has to be realistic. A wolf would never behave like that. Never!"*

With the recap of the McDonald's wolf story ready to email, I looked down at my throbbing, swollen, bandaged leg, shook my head, and pressed the "send" button.

Unreal!

Chapter 2

ICHABOD CRANE

Never judge a book by its cover
Author Unknown

So, there I was at the local Costco in Ogden, signing copies of my book, *A Train to Potevka.* On the table before me was the usual large stack of books, which I was busily personalizing for the group of people that had gathered there waiting in line.

As the number of people began to dwindle, my eyes took me straight ahead, twenty to thirty feet away, directly towards the area where Costco's frozen foods are kept. Standing there next to the freezer full of New York cheesecake, was an old man: tall, skinny, and noticeably worn. His most distinctive feature was his large, pointed, handsome nose. Looking at him, my mind immediately took me back to the classic Halloween story of Ichabod Crane and *The Legend of Sleepy Hollow*. This particular Ichabod, however, was staring directly at me—scowling.

Understandably, as a former covert agent, when you have an Ichabod, or any "Bod" for that matter, watching you so intently, scowling, you follow your instincts and keep your eye on him.

After ten busy minutes, I had finally signed a book for everyone waiting in line. As the people cleared away, Ichabod slowly walked towards me, stopped at the edge of my table, reached down and picked up one of my books.

"You wrote this?" he asked in a firm but raspy voice.

"Yes, sir, I wrote the book. I'm Mike Ramsdell; I'm the author," I replied.

"And what's your book about?" he asked.

"The book is about some of my experiences during my years living and working in Russia as a counterintelligence agent."

Immediately he gave me that unmistakable look of disbelief.

"So, you from back East or from the West Coast?"

"No, sir," I said. "I was born and raised right here in the Rocky Mountains of northern Utah."

"Northern Utah? Where in northern Utah?" he asked suspiciously.

"If you're from this area, sir, you've probably heard of the town where I grew up— Bear River. Actually Bear River City to be more correct," I added.

"I find that hard to believe," he exclaimed quite loudly. "How in the world could a person from a small town like Bear River City end up working as a covert agent in Russia?"

Giving him a quick, summarized version, I explained how I always had wanted to serve my country in the military like my dad and brothers; and, how, after seeing my first "007" movie—*From Russia With Love*—back when I was in college, I chose a path where I was eventually able to serve as a counterintelligence officer during my years with the military and other security agencies.

The entire time I was telling my story, Ichabod stared at me, slowly shaking his head from side to side in disbelief.

"You got to be pulling my leg," he chortled.

"No, sir, I'm not pulling your leg," I replied.

"Well, I've got just one question, Mr. Ernest Hemingway from Bear River City, how many books have you written?"

"Sir," I replied, watching him as he thumbed through the pages of my book, "this is my very first attempt at writing. It's my first book."

"Enough said!" he bellowed with a half chuckle, half snort. And with that he slammed the copy he was holding of *A Train to Potevka* down on the table loudly enough to startle a nearby couple browsing through the book stacks. Promptly, he walked off towards the Costco exit, still shaking his head and muttering to himself.

I watched as old Ichy disappeared among the crowd of Costco shoppers thinking to myself,

You old goat! You make fun of me by comparing me to Ernest Hemingway, but even he, too, had to start somewhere.

Not long after the incident, I had another group of people gathered in front of me; and, again, I was busy signing books.

After 30 minutes, I had totally forgotten about weird Ichabod. Then, while handing a personalized book to a young lady, one of the last people in line, I was taken aback—there directly behind her stood Ichabod.

When the crowd was totally gone, Ichabod approached my table, grabbed one of my books and said,

"Mr. Ramsdell, while walking around the store,"—probably while making his daily rounds for the free Costco samples—"I remembered that Costco has a policy (which, by the way, is true) that no matter how long you've had something you bought from Costco, you can return it for a full refund with no questions asked."

I knew right away where this conversation was going.

"So, Mr. Ramsdell, I'm going to buy your book; but I'll do it only on the condition that you tell me where you're signing tomorrow."

I was surprised by his comment.

"With all due respect, sir, what has where I'm signing tomorrow got to do with you buying my book?" I asked.

"Because after buying your book, I'm gonna take it home and tonight I'm gonna read the first chapter. And if it's a piece of junk, I want to know where you are signing tomorrow so I can deliver it back to you personally."

What a doodle!

Each fall when Halloween comes around, I had always enjoyed reading the story or watching the Disney adaption of *The Legend of Sleepy Hollow* and Ichabod Crane. However, I was definitely not enjoying the lanky, gaunt version of Ichabod standing now in front of me. What a grouch!

I pulled my signing schedule from my briefcase, looked it over, and told Ichabod that I would be signing the next day at the Costco in Bountiful from 10 AM until 6 PM.

"But, in truth, sir, I hope I won't see you there tomorrow; it's a fifty-mile round trip drive," I said, trying to make a joke with him. But he just shrugged his shoulders, tucked my book under his arm, and headed for the Costco cash registers.

There are certainly some strange folks in this world, I thought to myself, watching Ichy disappear. However, I was determined that this grump was not going to ruin the rest of my day or the upcoming weekend.

Gladly, more customers were soon in line at my table where I kept busy greeting people and signing books for the remainder of the day until 6:00 PM.

While driving home on the freeway, I noticed a tall, old man walking along the nearby frontage road. The sight took me back to my strange Costco encounter with an even stranger Ichabod. I couldn't help but wonder to myself, *Would Ichy really read my book?*

Bonnie had dinner waiting when I arrived home. As we ate, I told her about my day and my confrontation with odd Ichabod. Typical of Bonnie, rather than think of him as weird, like I did, she was concerned about him based on my description of his skinny physical condition, his old age, and shabby dress. She worried that he might be in need of some sort of help.

"Maybe he's not doing well. Did you think to ask if there was anything you could do for him?" she queried.

"Gee," I countered, "he has enough money for a Costco membership and can obviously afford my newest Hemingway novel. Not to worry, he's okay."

Ichabod didn't cross my mind the rest of the evening.

The next morning, I showered, shaved, and dressed. I grabbed a quick bowl of Frosted Flakes; kissed Bon goodbye; bid *paka* to our three cats Gorbachev, Yeltsin, and Putin; and headed down I-15 to the Bountiful Costco. Arriving twenty minutes early, I set up my posters and stacked my table with books, anticipating a busy Saturday of signing autographs.

With everything ready, at 10 AM I sat down in my chair. Just as I did, I looked towards the Costco front entrance. As the doors went up, who was the first person I saw striding purposefully toward me? None other than crotchety Ichabod Crane.

Oh boy, I thought. *Now what's going to happen?*

Dressed in the same set of worn clothes as the day before, Ichabod was one of the first customers, if not the very first, in the store.

Not at all knowing what was about to happen, I quickly tried to think of what I was going to say. I stood up from my chair. As I watched Ichabod walk towards me, I decided I was not going to let Mr. Grumpy embarrass me in front of other customers or get in the first word about how bad my book was or how terrible my writing skills were.

Ten feet away from me, with my book clutched in one hand, he opened his mouth to speak.

"Sir," I said hurriedly, "this has never happened before. I apologize. If you'll just take the book over to Costco Customer Service, they will gladly refund your money."

He hesitated momentarily, as if he had been caught off guard by my words.

He looked directly at me, " . . . But . . . but that's not the problem!" he said.

"Well then . . . so what's the problem?" I asked, waiting for the complaints to begin.

"The problem is, Mr. Ramsdell, I haven't been to bed!" he said, as a big grin appeared across his face.

Speechless, I stood looking at him. Did I really understand what I thought he had said . . .

that, maybe—perhaps—he actually *had* read my book . . . and liked it?

My new best friend, Ichabod, proceeded to buy 270 books!

After several minutes of getting over the shock and realizing that he *really* was going to purchase 270 books, I walked to the aisle where Costco sells office chairs and rolled one of the more plush, comfortable-looking ones back and placed it at the table, next to mine. Ichabod sat next to me as I began the task of personalizing the first 100 books—all that the Bountiful Costco had in stock at the time. As I signed, I questioned Ichabod about his life, his family, where he lived, his career, etc. This was my new best friend. I wanted to know everything about him.

In my five years of doing book signings for Costco across the western United States, the most books I have ever signed at any given event was 640. This happened six months after *A Train to Potevka* was first released at the Costco flagship warehouse in Issaquah, Washington. That night, after the Issaquah signing, I could hardly hold my toothbrush. I was thrilled beyond words. But, *never* had I sold 270 books to one individual—not even close!

As we visited, Ichabod told me he was from the Weber County area, had raised a large family, and now had dozens of grandchildren and great-grandchildren. Regrettably, his wife of sixty-some years had passed away only months earlier. He admitted that being alone without her was a struggle, one of the most difficult things he had ever done.

Our conversation about his wife lead him to ask endless questions about my own wife, Bonnie, and our love story which I write about in *Potevka*. Several times I had to laugh when he kept referring to me as "Blockhead" because of my years of unwillingness to get involved with Bonnie due to my failed first marriage.

"Didn't you see what was right there in front of you while Bonnie was hitting you over the head, trying to get your attention?! Man, what were you thinking?" He gave me a bad time, but was happy for me just the same.

When I questioned him about buying so many books, he said he had spent his career in construction and had been fortunate enough to own his own company, and a very successful one at that. He was now retired; the company was run by his four sons. He wanted a book for each of them, each of his daughters, and all his grandchildren and great-grandchildren. And he wanted a book for each of his company's clients.

After I had signed the first one hundred books, we agreed that I would finish the remaining 170 over the next few days and he would pick them up at another time at his convenience.

What a remarkable man and what a remarkable experience.

And the moral of the story: even as an author, you can never judge a book—or a dear old, frumpy, crotchety Ichabod—by its cover.

Chapter 3

ABDUL'S AMERICA

Goodness is richer than greatness. It consists not in the outward things we do, but in the inward thing we are.

Edwin Hubbel Chapin

Growing up in my small home town of Bear River—three hundred families, give or take a few—the only times I remember getting the chance to venture out of that small world was just twice a year. One was for the annual summer fishing trip with my dad and four older brothers to the Greys River in Wyoming. The other occasion was during the Christmas holidays when Dad would take Mom, my older sister, Karen, and me to Salt Lake City where we would stay overnight—always at the Hotel

Little on Main Street. Our stay was for one night only and usually during the week before Christmas. For a young country boy from the so-called sticks, staying in a hotel overnight in the big city was magical.

Because of my family's financial situation, there were few purchases—mostly window shopping. When I think back on my Christmases as a youth, that one day and night spent in Salt Lake during the holidays is a treasured memory: the huge department stores of Auerbach's and ZCMI, Temple Square, the giant Tribune Christmas tree, and the entire city decorated with multi-colored lights.

As a boy, my family didn't have television; so the only time I had exposure to the outside world, other than the annual fishing and holiday excursion, was from the textbooks and picture books we read in school.

During the summer before my senior year of high school, our school choir—I sang with the tenors—toured the Northwest for a week. As a member of the well-known Bear River High School Choir, I traveled with my classmates and best friends through Idaho, Oregon, Washington, and British Columbia where we performed concerts in various communities along the way. One hundred teenagers packed in two large buses, traveling together out of state—we definitely thought we had arrived.

Of course, we stopped to see all the special points of interest along the way.

Many of my classmates had already traveled to such places in the Western states, so I had to temper my excitement as a teenager, I couldn't appear too enthusiastic. With my nose pressed up against the window of that big motor coach, I sat in my seat watching the cities, towns, and wide open spaces of Northwest America pass by. I was fascinated by these places I had only heard about or seen in photographs.

I remember promising myself, after that first exposure to traveling, that when I became an adult I would have a career that would allow me to visit all fifty states. It was in those early years with my high school choir that the travel bug bit me and never let go.

While in college, I took time away from my schooling to serve an LDS mission to Germany. My specific mission area included southern Germany and northern Switzerland. I fell in love with the people, their culture, their languages, and especially . . . with their food.

Once my mission was complete, I returned back home to the United States with a new promise to myself of someday living and working abroad. Because of those two years in Europe, back at the university, I changed my major to political science with an emphasis on international studies.

After graduation from Utah State, I was accepted to law school at the University of Utah. Having completed half of my law degree, I received orders from the military to report for active duty. It was at officer's basic training at Fort Knox, Kentucky that, along with other members of my battalion, I took a battery of tests to determine my competence in various academic disciplines. Because of my mission languages, I was fortunate to score high marks in the language portion of the exams.

Prior to my years in postgraduate law studies, I had already received my commission as an officer in the Military Intelligence Corps, which eventually led to my acceptance into the Russian Studies/Russian Language program in Washington, D.C.

I'd always had a special interest in this other world superpower—Russia. After reporting for school in D.C., I was informed that my course work did not actually begin for another few weeks. Therefore, I took advantage of this down time to experience as much of Washington, D.C. as possible. During those weeks, I fell in love with our nation's capital and the surrounding areas of Virginia, Pennsylvania, Delaware, Maryland, and New York, where so much of our nation's history had its beginnings. For a young officer in the military, it was an exciting time to be living in Washington, D.C., in the heart of America at the epicenter of both political and military power around the world.

One of the most memorable experiences of my life took place the night I first arrived in Washington, D.C. to report for school. It was almost midnight, the end of January. A winter storm had left a six-inch blanket of new snow along the East Coast before turning out to the Atlantic. Because of the storm and late hour, there was very little traffic and few people in the city.

As most visitors know, the must-see sights of D.C.—the massive government buildings, the beautiful parks, the famous monuments—are in very close proximity to one another. I had driven all day from Fort Knox, Kentucky. As I came off the freeway, crossed the Potomac River, and looked towards the end of the bridge on which I was driving, I could see a huge, lighted structure. As the road circled around it, I realized it was the magnificent Lincoln Memorial. My whole life I had dreamed of someday visiting this sacred place.

The parking lot was completely empty when I pulled in. I parked my car, put on my military jacket and headgear, and walked through the snow towards the memorial. As I climbed the steps, I could hardly breathe because of the solemn moment. It was as if President Lincoln sat up there beckoning me to come and stand near him.

When I got up to the last step, I looked to my right, then to my left. With the exception of a single national park ranger, at that late hour I was the only person in the entire sacred place.

With the snow gently falling, I stood in awe of the man and the moment. For me, President Lincoln has always been the greatest of our nation's leaders. Whenever asked who it would be if I could go back in time and have a conversation with someone, I always answer that I would want it to be President Lincoln.

As I had done so many times before, this night, again, I read the stirring words of this humble man's Gettysburg Address. At that moment, it seemed I could feel the pain and anguish President Lincoln must have suffered as he struggled to keep our nation together.

I admit I have had few spiritual experiences in my life. However, that hour I spent alone at the Lincoln Memorial—along with my first visit to the hallowed grounds of our military cemetery in Normandy, France—will always remain close to my heart.

Due to the demands of Russian Language School—a one-and-a-half-year accelerated program that gave us the equivalent of a master's degree in Russian Studies and Russian Language—I had very little free time. However, I took what few opportunities I had to visit our national treasures: the Smithsonian, the Air and Space Museum, the Museum of National History, and, my favorite—the National Gallery of Art. I cannot think of a time when I've ever visited Washington, D.C. since and not paid a visit to see our nation's priceless collections of art.

I sometimes catch myself lamenting that our nation's capital is not more centrally located in the middle of our country so more of our citizens could have the opportunity to experience our national treasures—past and present.

Once I graduated from the Russian Institute and my active duty career started, I was assigned as an instructor to the U.S. Intelligence School-Europe, located in Oberammergau in southern Germany. The day I received my orders, I was thrilled beyond words. I loved my two years in Germany as a missionary. Now I was going back as a member of the military to serve in one of the

41

most beautiful, picturesque areas in all of Europe.

During my years teaching at the school, I took every opportunity to see as much of Europe as I could: France, Italy, Spain, Holland, England, and Austria. There is something magical about Europe; so much history, so much to see, and so much to experience. Early in my career I decided that, if at all possible, I would take every opportunity to someday be assigned back to Europe while working for the government or for a multi-national firm.

After my initial tour of duty in Europe, I returned to the States where I had the chance to visit much of America as part of my work responsibilities. After a few years back in the USA, I once again was able to use my language skills and covert training by serving as an intelligence officer in Europe, Scandinavia, and Russia.

The big break in my career came when the KGB compromised our new American Embassy in Moscow, Russia, during its construction. The compromise of our embassy and my subsequent work there is at the heart of my book, *A Train to Potevka*.

During the years I was assigned to Moscow, I also had an apartment in Helsinki, Finland, the closest Western capital to Moscow, 1000 kilometers away. While living part of the time in Helsinki, the countries of Scandinavia began to feel like a second home—Denmark, Norway, Sweden, and Finland. My own family heritage—Ramsdell on my father's side and Anderson on my mother's side—originated from Scandinavia. The majority of Bear River, the small town where I grew up, was settled by Scandinavian immigrants. Therefore, it must be in my bloodline, because I felt a strong connection with the people and the cultures of Northern Europe. They are a wonderful, dedicated, and hard working people. I'm proud to claim my lineage from them.

Once I retired and my career was over, Bonnie and I left Russia and Scandinavia and returned to America, back home to the Rocky Mountains. Soon we were busy re-establishing relationships with family and friends and building our new home. Although I was called back to Russia and Finland from time to time during the construction of our home, we did very little traveling, especially here in the States. Once our home was finally built and we had moved in, we wanted to take a break from the demands of how busy we had been and get away by doing some traveling stateside.

About the only place we had never visited in America was the Northeast. Thus, when fall began to roll around, we decided the time was right to make the pilgrimage to see the fall colors of New England. Over the years, hearing so much about the beauty there in the fall, I'd often wondered if it really could hold up in comparison to a drive through the canyons of the Rocky Mountains during the peak of the colors in late September.

During my early years as a lieutenant stationed in southern Germany, it had been a dream of mine to one day own a Volkswagen camper. The appeal of mobility, convenience, and adventure all combined in one automobile made it the perfect all-around vehicle. But strangely, it wasn't until I left Germany and returned home to America that I achieved my goal.

Not long after returning from Europe, I bought a used 1972, Volkswagen pop-top camper, the kind that allows for an additional sleeping compartment above the lower level. My boy, Chris, and I affectionately named it the Mus Bus because of its mustard yellow color. It was like a second home to me and Chris. It served as a school bus some mornings, a team bus during football season, a ski shuttle in the winter, and as a hotel-on-wheels in the summer when it took us to our favorite nearby places:

up Logan Canyon to Ram Station, Bear Lake, and beautiful Jackson Hole, Wyoming.

After Bonnie and I returned home from my assignment in Russia, from time to time we were called back to the agency in Washington, D.C. As these trips began to occur with some regularity, we made the decision to drive our VW camper across the country, while visiting, of course, the tourist sites along the way, and then leave the vehicle in long-term parking at Andrews Air Force Base outside of Washington. Thus, when flying back and forth between Utah and D.C., we always had our Mus Bus to use—our own condo-on-wheels.

One beautiful fall, Bonnie and I spent two perfect weeks driving our Mus Bus along the highways and byways of New England: Connecticut, Massachusetts, New Hampshire, Vermont, and Maine. The brilliant blue skies provided the perfect backdrop for the endless fall hues of the Northeast. The grandeur of the pallet of colors would at times seem to take one's breath away. After spending two weeks there, we simply did not want the trip to end.

When we left New England, we headed south to Manhattan, where we planned to spend a few days before driving the Mus Bus to Andrews Air Force Base in Washington, D.C. and flying back to Utah. Along with seeing the sights of New York, the U.S. Open Tennis Championships were being played at Flushing Meadows.

I was first introduced to tennis during my years in law school. I immediately became a big fan of the sport and tried to play whenever my studies would allow. Earlier, while living in Europe, I'd been able to attend Wimbledon in England and the French Open in Paris—two of the four major championships; the others being the Australian Open in Melbourne, and our own U.S. Championships held every fall at Flushing Meadows in New York. Thus, while in New York, Bonnie and I were able to attend the men's final where Lleyton Hewitt of Australia upset America's Pete Sampras to win the championship at the year's last major tournament.

The agreement I had made with Bonnie was that if she would attend the tennis matches with me, in turn, I would get tickets for us to see one of the musicals playing on Broadway. The day after the tennis championship was Monday. As New York theater-goers know, Mondays are always dark. It's the one day of the week when no shows play on Broadway—Family Home Evening in New York City. . . . Yeh, right!

As Bonnie can attest, when you travel with Mike Ramsdell, you'd better have your sneakers laced on tight, because I tend to go a hundred miles an hour. I want to visit every tourist site, see every landmark, visit every museum; I want to see it all.

Tuesday, our last full day in New York, I was already up, dressed, and ready to go when Bonnie said she'd had enough of my breakneck pace. She wanted to catch a few more hours of sleep. So, out the door I went with my camera and New York travel guide in hand. I hustled around the vicinity of where we were staying, taking pictures of the area and of the beautiful panoramic views of downtown New York. Probably an hour had passed before I returned to join Bonnie. While sitting on the edge of the bed, we heard a louder-than-usual noise. Not to worry, this is New York—traffic, horns, sirens, and noise, noise, noise.

While discussing our plans for our last day in New York—what sights we would visit, what museums we would see, and where we would eat dinner before our eight-o'clock show time at the theater (we were planning to see "Lion King")—again, another loud noise erupted and jolted the bed. Sensing something was different than the normal deafening sounds of New York, I told Bonnie to stay put while I went to see what was happening.

Once outside, I looked towards the city skyline; the terrorists had just flown the second plane into the second tower.

As the sky turned black from the smoke of the burning jet fuel, time seemed to stand still. The moment was surreal. My very first reaction was that I was seeing a movie set, that some Hollywood film studio was shooting a film. This couldn't possibly be real.

Bonnie quickly dressed and joined me outside. We kept looking to the skies, worried that New York, and possibly the entire country, was under attack. As we witnessed the destruction and smelled the smoke, it seemed as if we could actually feel the heat from the burning structures and jet fuel. To see the panic and chaos of that moment is a memory which will stay with us forever.

A major communication and technology hub, most of New York's ability to relay information went down with the Twin Towers. While the rest of America and the world watched and waited, the area of greater New York was basically without communications. This prevented us from knowing about the severity of the attacks or the subsequent attack on the Pentagon and the plane that had gone down in Pennsylvania.

Realizing that our families and friends knew we were in New York, we tried desperately to notify them that we were okay. However, with the main antennas which had been on top of the

World Trade Towers now destroyed, it was impossible to make contact with anyone.

Almost as quickly as the terrorist attacks happened, police and security appeared throughout the city and entire area. No sooner did I have my camera out taking photos of the burning towers, than police appeared out of nowhere to check our identification papers. Other security personnel began to inspect the surrounding structures for possible explosives and other terrorist activity.

We were directed by the security police to return to our hotel and informed that New York City and the surrounding suburbs were going to be locked down. With no way to get in touch with our families, Bonnie and I made the decision to try to make it out of New York via the military facility at Fort Wadsworth on Staten Island. Luckily, using our military papers and identification, we were allowed to leave the area.

Once we got on the New Jersey Turnpike, our intention was to drive to Washington, D.C., where we hoped to be able to catch a flight from the East Coast back home to Salt Lake City. As we drove south on the freeway, we encountered very little traffic going in our direction. The northbound freeway, however, was an endless caravan of police vehicles, ambulances, paramedic trucks, and other emergency vehicles headed to New York.

Finally out of the New York area and able to use the phone, we made contact with our families to let them know we were okay.

Once we learned of the severity of the attacks and the massive destruction at Ground Zero, Bonnie and I made the decision to return to New York, hoping we could be of use to the rescue effort. When we got back to Fort Wadsworth, we reported to the base commander to offer our help. The following day we were assigned to the Home Port Rescue Center where hundreds of firemen, rescue workers, and police lived during the months of recovering the bodies from under the mountain of rubble.

The rescue center was manned and fully operational within twenty-four hours after the attacks. For those of us assigned there as volunteers, it was our responsibility to take care of all the needs of the rescue workers: maintain their dorm rooms, help prepare their meals, do their washing, and anything else they needed. We worked in eight-hour shifts on a three-day cycle: the first day we would help unload semis in the warehouse (the very first eighteen wheeler we unloaded was full of dog food for the rescue dogs); the second day we worked in the cafeteria; and each third day—strange as it may sound—we were asked to attend funerals.

With so many fallen firefighters and policemen pulled from the rubble, some days there were as many as four or five funerals. With all his responsibilities as Mayor of New York City, Rudy Giuliani spoke at each and every funeral. On September 11, 343 firemen died trying to save the lives of others from the burning towers. Most funerals Bonnie and I attended for the firemen began with an American flag-draped coffin on a fire truck followed by a large, solemn entourage of fellow firefighters—a moving tribute to America's heroes of 9/11.

Working as volunteers at the Rescue Center was a constant reminder of the pain, suffering, and devastation the terrorists had caused. Having personally witnessed the destruction at Ground Zero, it was very hard to comprehend the great hatred and callous disregard the terrorists had for 3,000 innocent civilians. And to think, the attacks happened right here on American soil. September 11, 2001 was the deadliest day in our nation's history. We lost more lives that day than the attacks on Pearl Harbor and on D-Day.

The events of 9/11 broke America's heart, but they did not break our nation's spirit. That day was, also, a day of great heroism and a lasting legacy to the men and women who continue to serve to keep America safe.

After having been away from our home in the Rockies for almost three months, Bonnie and I felt it was time to return home, grateful for the opportunity we'd had to help our country, and specifically New York, at the time of this terrible tragedy. When we notified the authorities of our decision to leave, the kind people at the Home Port Rescue Center honored us with a small ceremony in recognition of our service.

For the months we'd been on the East Coast, we had used our Volkswagen van not only for transportation, but also as our living quarters while working at the Rescue Center. The entire time our old VW had performed almost flawlessly, as if it had just come off the showroom floor thirty-plus years earlier in Stuttgart, Germany. Then, unexpectedly, a few days prior to leaving New York to set out on our 2,500-mile drive across America, our ever-reliable, VW camper began to have problems.

The day before we were to leave, we determined there was no way we could risk setting off on such a long journey with the bus in such poor running condition. We were in big trouble: our thirty-year old Volkswagen was in need of serious mechanical repairs and there we

were in greater New York, one of the most
expensive cities in the world. I couldn't begin
to imagine what the repair bill would be.

Not knowing of any repair garage in the
city, I visited the base commander and told him
of our problem. Without hesitation,
Commander Jewkes took a piece of paper from
his desk and copied down an address from his
Rolodex. He also pulled out a street map and
outlined travel directions with a felt tip marker.

"When you get there, Mike, ask for Abdul,"
he said. "He will help you, and he'll be fair
with the repair costs."

I thanked him and walked out of his office,
concerned not with the location of the repair
garage, but with the name . . . Abdul.

*Just who exactly is this, with a name like
that? But then,* I thought, *this is New York, the
melting pot of the world.*

The following day we were up early and ate
breakfast, studying the map Commander
Jewkes had given us. I drove while Bonnie
played navigator. Down this street and that
street, around this corner and that corner, all the
while worrying about the extent of the needed
repairs and what the cost would be.

After twenty minutes, we found the address
and stopped the Mus Bus in front of a huge,
asphalt-covered lot. The place was entirely
encircled with 12-foot high steel fencing with

multiple strands of razor wire at the top. Inside were several old cars, all seemingly in need of repairs. In the middle of the lot was the garage with tools, equipment, and car engines scattered round about.

"This can't be the place," I said to Bonnie. "This looks more like a prison."

She showed me the address on the slip of paper Commander Jewkes had given us; it matched the address on the sign hanging from the huge, reinforced steel gate.

As we discussed whether to stay or drive away, a door at the side of the garage opened; a short, stocky, middle-aged man walked towards us. When he reached the gate, he removed a set of keys from his coveralls and began to undo the several locks on the gate. Once finished, the man pulled the heavy gate open and motioned for us to drive inside. When I cleared the gate, I took the Mus Bus out of gear, pulled on the emergency brake, and jumped out to greet him.

"My name is Mike Ramsdell. I'm having problems with my VW bus. Commander Jewkes at the Home Port Rescue Center said you could possibly help me."

The man was obviously of Middle Eastern descent, approximately 45 years old, medium build, with dark hair and a full beard. He acted like he knew why I was there. He motioned with his hands for me to get back in my bus and follow him. Once he got close to the garage building, he held his up hand for me to stop.

"You . . . there," he said in his broken English, pointing to two old car seats next to the side of the building. "You sit, we fix."

Suddenly four other Middle Eastern men came out of the garage all dressed in dirty, greasy coveralls, mumbling their strange language to one another. Two of them kept staring at Bonnie, which made me very uncomfortable. The four men addressed the man who had opened the gate as Abdul. By their interaction, it was obvious that Abdul was the boss.

"Sorry, sir, me no mechanic. Bus no run," I told him while gesturing with my arms and using jerky body movements to demonstrate how my vehicle was behaving.

The five Arabs stood looking at me, mumbling to one another. I'm sure they were saying, "This American is crazy."

The two car seats Abdul offered us would place us out of sight while they did the repairs.

"No way am I going to let that happen," I whispered to Bonnie.

I could envision them pulling out my engine and replacing it with an even worse piece of junk or stripping the vehicle of parts that I wouldn't know were missing until it was too late. Against Abdul's request, I instructed Bonnie to get back in the passenger seat and to stay there.

"I'll stand outside while they do the repairs to make sure they don't steal anything. And make certain that I can see you at all times," I said to her.

I could tell that she, too, was becoming as uncomfortable and concerned as I was.

Abdul pulled open the engine door and directed one of his workers to start the motor. They took turns kneeling at the back of the van, sticking their heads inside the engine compartment trying to determine the problem. They jabbered away in their raspy language with one another, obviously arguing about what the problem was and how it should be fixed.

I stood behind them, ten or fifteen feet away, worried about the volume of their arguing, wondering if it would eventually lead to blows. Every now and again, when one of them would make a loud statement, they would all turn and look at me, then laugh and laugh. After an hour and a half, I was beginning to realize I had made a big mistake. I approached Abdul.

"Sir, sorry for problem," I said. "Better me take Volkswagen to New York dealership."

Abdul looked at me, then said something to his workers; again, they all broke out laughing.

The only words I caught were "two thousand dollars."

I was ready to put an end to this circus with Abdul and his Arab brothers when, again, he pointed towards the car seats.

"You sit, we fix, " he said.

What am I doing here? I thought.

Why would Commander Jewkes send me to a repair garage run by a bunch of arrogant, Middle Eastern thugs. Most of all, my mind couldn't let go of the moment when, almost three months earlier, with my very eyes I saw the destruction these men's brothers had caused our country: the deaths, the lifelong disabilities, the pain, the ruin, the cost. Dressed in their Middle Eastern headgear and speaking their strange language, no wonder they had razor wire surrounding their facility. The razor wire was probably not there to keep thieves out; it was more than likely there to protect them. How ashamed they had to be to show themselves in public after what their fellow Arabs had done to America.

While Abdul worked tirelessly in and around the engine compartment; his workers carried tools and parts back and forth from the garage. I didn't budge. Standing fifteen feet away, I watched their every move, and I wanted them to know I was watching.

Finally, after four hours, Abdul stood up and walked to the driver's side of the van, opened the door, and sat down.

When seated, he looked out the window at me, "Now okay," he said.

I told Bonnie to get out of the Mus Bus. Abdul fired up the engine, and, instead of sounding like a bucket of rocks, the engine began to purr. Bonnie and I looked at one another.

"But will it run once it's in gear?" I said to her, still disbelieving that this motley crew knew what they were doing.

After an additional four or five minutes of them adjusting the carburetor, Abdul motioned for me to get in.

"You drive," he said, holding the door for me to get in. "You test."

"This fool wants me to do a test drive," I said in a whisper to Bonnie, "Get in. Let's get out of here while we can."

Bonnie got in the passenger seat, shut the door, and pulled on her seat belt.

"You're not going to do what I think you're going to do, are you?" she said.

"I just want to get out of this place," I said emphatically. "These dopes are stupid enough to let us go do a test drive."

Abdul walked towards the huge metal gate, opened the locks, and motioned for us to drive through.

"You test," he said, as I slowly passed through the gate.

As I drove onto the street, I went from first gear to second, to third, to fourth. The engine hummed like it had when I first bought it. It had been years since it had such power and acceleration. How could they have done this? I had always believed that their lives, their culture, and their country were so messed up—one big debacle. But here were at least five Arabs who, apparently, knew how to fix Volkswagen engines. How could that be?

After all the pain and sorrow Bonnie and I had witnessed in New York because of what the Arab terrorists had done, it did cross my mind to keep on driving. I told myself,

Once back home in Utah, I will send them a check for the repairs.

"You know you have to go back," Bonnie said.

Once again, she knew exactly what I was thinking.

"But . . ."

"Mike, come on. This isn't like you. You know that if you don't go back, you'll always regret it."

"But . . . how much will they expect to be paid? Yes, Abdul did most of the work, but the four others helped him."

She just looked at me.

"It doesn't matter," she replied. "You have to go back."

The Mus Bus was almost like a first born child. My thirty-year-old Volkswagen was now purring like a kitten. But I still didn't want to go back.

With Bonnie navigating, we drove the four or five miles back to the garage. Waiting at the entrance, there stood Abdul ready to open the gate. His workers stood near the garage looking surprised, as if they, too, knew what I had been thinking regarding my escape.

Once inside, I stopped the van, grabbed my briefcase and stepped out towards Abdul. From my wallet, I pulled out my American Express card and offered it to Abdul. He looked up at me, shaking his head.

"No pay," he said.

"American Express no work? I have Visa. Okay?" I said.

"No," Abdul said as he gestured with his hand, rejecting the cards.

"Wait," I said, then hurriedly got into the vehicle to explain to Bonnie the problem we were having.

"These Arab cowboys don't take American Express or Visa," I said to Bonnie. "We might be in trouble. How much cash do you have?"

Bonnie counted the bills in her purse. I found $55 dollars in my wallet. Together we had $104 dollars.

"What are we going to do?" she asked.

"There's no way they'll take my word that we'll come back in the morning with more money. And there's no dang way we are staying in the bus, parked here overnight in this ghetto." I replied.

Frantic, I used my cell phone to call Commander Jewkes at his office, but he had gone for the rest of the day.

"You stay here," I told Bonnie. "I'll give it another try. Maybe he'll be reasonable with us."

As I got out of the van, I looked at my new Citizen watch—the one my son had given me the prior Christmas. Perhaps, I could convince Abdul to hold it as collateral.

Getting more uncomfortable and worried, I stood in front of Abdul.

"Sir," I said, "You take $104 dollars and new Citizen watch now. The rest in the morning. Tomorrow morning I pay the rest."

With his workers looking on, again, Abdul shook his head from side to side.

"No. No pay," he said.

Getting more anxious with each passing minute, I said,

"Abdul, very sorry, but always I pay with credit card. Today you take money and watch. Tomorrow I pay rest. Okay?"

There was no way I was going to let them play this out to have us leave our vehicle with them overnight.

Again I offered him the cash; I even counted out the bills this time and took the watch off of my wrist.

Again, Abdul refused to take them.

"You no pay," he said, shaking his head.

I was getting more and more frustrated. This negotiation was going nowhere!

"Abdul, we have problem," I said, irritably. "Sorry for my trouble to you. But, I offer credit cards—you say no! I offer $104 dollars and wristwatch—you say no! Man . . . do you understand my English?! I want to pay! You work many hours. My car now perfect. I want to pay!"

The moment became very awkward; everything seemed to stop. It was as if Abdul wanted to tell me something. Unexpectedly, he stepped towards me, put his hand on my shoulder, and motioned for me to follow him.

"Come, Mr. Mike," he said. The calm tone in his voice began to ease the fear and anxiety I had been experiencing since arriving at his repair garage several hours earlier.

"Bonnie," I said, "just stay here in the Mus Bus. I'll be right back, Abdul has something to show me"

I followed Abdul as we made our way to the other side of the garage. When he stopped, he turned and pointed in the direction of lower Manhattan where, weeks earlier, the World Trade Towers had been. From where the two of us stood, we had a perfect view.

"Morning of 9/11," he said, "we hear first plane—boom! Fifteen minutes, second plane—boom!"

Then, after a long pause, "My wife work 60th floor, second tower. . . . I see my wife die."

Tears welled in his eyes.

I stood speechless.

"Me, wife, two little boys come to America for one thing—freedom. Now all gone. No more dreams," he said, choking on his words.

I stood without speaking, trying to imagine what he, too, had suffered that terrible day because of terrorists from his very own country.

"I go crazy," he continued, "I climb fence and run. I run and run and run.

"I scream, 'I hate God! I hate America. Why? Why? Why?' Two boys, now no mother. I run and run. On bridge"—he pointed to the massive Verrazano Bridge off in the distance—"I hear cell phone, my cell phone. I stop running. I pull phone from coveralls, 'Hello, hello,' I say. Then . . . a voice . . . 'Abdul, Abdul, I'm alive, I'm okay. I made it out. Abdul,' she said me, 'go to school, get our boys. Meet me at home.'"

With tears flowing down his checks into his thick, dark beard, and with tears also running down my ashamed face, we stood looking at one another. Without saying a word, Abdul and I embraced, sharing both the sorrow and the joy of that terrible day of 9/11.

Finally, we separated, each with a greater appreciation for what we had in common rather than our differences.

"Mr. Mike," he said, "you here to help us, to help New York. Me no chance to help because who I am, my language, how I look—me Arab. But you, you broke Volkswagen, I help you. Now. . . understand? You no pay!"

During the next several days, as Bonnie and I drove our smooth-running VW across America, how proud I was to see the thousands of American flags atop buildings and bridges, schools and businesses, at truck stops and service stations, on buses and semis, and on thousands upon thousands of automobiles along the roads and highways of our country.

While traveling the 2,500 miles home, I couldn't help but think of our 9/11 experience in New York and, especially, I couldn't help but be reminded of Abdul—a man who had waited for 12 years to come to the USA to be able to raise his family in freedom, to one day become a U.S. citizen, and to enjoy the liberties and blessings so few of us truly appreciate.

September 11, 2001 changed America and the world forever. It certainly changed me, as did a humble, Middle Eastern auto mechanic who reminded me, once again, about the innate goodness of all God's children.

May God bless our United States of America.

TIPPING POINTS

COACH

A NOBLE SEA DOG

A LESSON IN CHARACTER

HEALING THE HEART

Chapter 4

COACH

*Our future is in our hands. Our lives are
what we choose to make them.*

Winston Churchill

Growing up a teenager in Bear River Valley
it was expected—actually a rite of passage—for
a young man to play on the high school football
team. My older brothers had been athletes.
Dee had been an outstanding Golden Gloves
boxer. Ted was selected to the All-State
football team while playing at Box Elder High
and later went on to play football at Utah State
University where he was captain of the Aggie
team his senior year.

Thus, the pressure was on me to follow in
my brothers' footsteps. However, I had a
serious problem. When I reported for football
my freshman year, I was five foot, six inches,

and didn't even weigh a hundred pounds—skinny as a rail.

I will never forget my first day of football practice. After we were given those strange-looking pads and equipment, we fumbled around trying to figure out what went where and just what body parts the pads were designed to protect. Nevertheless, I was thrilled to be on the team with my best friends.

I gave a hundred percent each afternoon at practice, but because of my size, I often took quite a beating. The only thing I could really do was throw a tight spiral. Otherwise, I got hammered on a daily basis; especially when I had to quarterback the second team offense against the first team defense during scrimmage.

Not dressing for any of the JV games like some of the better freshman players did, and not getting much practice time during the week, halfway through the season I began to have doubts about my dream of being a high school quarterback. Because of the typical teenage peer pressure, I couldn't bring myself to admit to any of my teammates—let alone any of the coaches—that I was considering quitting the team. Several of my best friends were the first-string starters, but most weighed fifty to sixty pounds more than I did. I'm sure few of them gave little thought or even realized the trouncing I was taking at each practice and how discouraged I was about not playing.

After a few more weeks of pain and punishment, I made the decision that I was going to meet with Coach Simmons and resign from the team.

On one particular afternoon during practice, I asked Coach if it would be all right if I could talk to him in his office when we were finished. I certainly didn't want to have such a discussion in front of my teammates.

Once practice was over and we had showered and dressed, my teammates loaded onto the two athletic buses for their early evening ride home. Because of my pending meeting with Coach, I would not be able to take the bus home as usual, but would hitchhike or bum a ride for the ten miles from the high school down to Bear River where my family lived.

As I walked to his office door, I remember being more scared and worried—mostly ashamed—than I had ever been. Finally, I gathered the courage to knock. A moment later, the door opened and Coach invited me in.

"Take a seat, Mike. So, what's on your mind?" he asked, as he offered a chair to me at the opposite side of his desk.

I fidgeted and squirmed awhile, trying to avoid what was coming.

"Coach," I said, "I'm sorry to bother you with this, but I've come to tell you that I think it's best I quit the football team."

"And why do you think that's the right decision?" he asked.

"Coach, I can't tell you how much I want to be a football player, especially like my brother Ted. Surely I have the desire, but I just don't have the size."

He seemed to look right through me as if he knew exactly where the conversation was going.

"Coach, I'm not making a contribution to our team, to my teammates, to you, or the rest of the coaching staff," I said. "Besides, I'm taking a pounding every afternoon at practice and getting the dog knocked out of me. Bottom line, I think it best that I quit the team."

As I waited for his response, I looked across the desk at this kind, gentle man. He was the last person I ever wanted to disappoint. He was truly a role model for each of us and treated me and the entire team with respect. It seemed like time stood still as I sat there across from the first man in my life who I felt truly cared about me as a person.

"Mike," he said, "I'm aware of your situation and the challenges you're going through. You come from a good family. You have great brothers and sisters. Your mother and dad have carried a heavy load with so many kids, but they've done the best they can. And even though your family probably never tells you, you need to understand something very important . . . you do have value. You are somebody; you have great things to accomplish in your life. It might not seem possible right now, but your life can be anything you want it to be. It's absolutely important that you realize you are not a quitter. If you quit this football team and don't see the season through, how much easier will it be to quit when faced with other challenges that, for certain, will come your way? And even more importantly—you don't quit on life! Sure, you don't have the size right now, but, I'm sure, your growth is yet to happen."

And then more of his encouraging words.

"Is there any other player on the team that can throw a football like you? Stay with us. Stay with the team and I promise you that eventually good things will happen."

I felt it wasn't hype or him just trying to make me feel good. I could tell he truly meant what he said.

As he stood to walk me to the door, to tell me goodbye, he reached out, pulled me towards him, gave me a hug, and told me how proud he was to call me a friend.

On that late fall afternoon, as if sent from heaven, that humble, wise man had touched my heart and told me exactly the words I needed to hear. There was no way I was going to leave the team. I was going to be there for every practice, still getting the dog knocked out of me every afternoon, but I was going to see the season through. But more important than just football, I had a renewed hope about who I was, my future, my dreams, and where this life might possibly take me.

As I look back on that experience, I am convinced that it had a great influence to help me make it through some of the difficulties and challenges that would come later in my life.

As an epilogue to this story, a few years later, as a senior, I was the starting varsity quarterback at Bear River High School. With several great players on our football team, we went through the season with only two losses, won the region championship, and made it to the state football playoffs for only the second time in our school's history. I weighed 128 pounds, but—by dang—could I throw the football!

Whenever I think back on that experience and how this man had such an influence on my life, I think of the great responsibility we have as adults—parents, grandparents, teachers, and leaders—to remind our young people that each of them has great value, that they are loved and needed, and that their lives can be a marvelous and rewarding journey.

I believe, like never before, our youth today are in need of heroes. Heroes like my very first mentor and high school football coach—Coach Gerald Simmons.

Thank you, Coach.

QB #15

Chapter 5

A NOBLE SEA DOG

The greater the man, the greater the courtesy.

Alfred Lord Tennyson

I have shared the following story with only a handful of people: my wife, Bonnie, my son, Chris, and a few close friends. You will understand why when you read this account of Mike Ramsdell and the "Monster" hidden within.

The incident of which you're about to read took place when I was a student at the Russian Language Institute in Washington, D.C. Words cannot express the pressure my classmates and I lived under for the year and a half we were assigned there.

The school was an old Naval facility building, at Anacostia Naval Station. It sat on the Potomac River, directly east of the National War College at Ft. McNair and just north of Bolling Air Force Base. Each of the professors in the Russian department were native Russians. They had a reputation for being demanding, demeaning, and seemed to have an ongoing contest with each other to see who could graduate the fewest students at the end of the 18-month course.

Vladimir Muzenchenko was the Russian instructor assigned to our class for the entire eighteen months. He was the exact twin of Russian Premier Nikita Kruschev, even down to the large gap between his front teeth. However, one noticeable difference between the two was that Khrushchev could often be seen with a smile. Muzenchenko, on the other hand, lived with a perpetual scowl that had permanently grown to his face.

Based on a program of total immersion, we students were expected to be fully engaged from day one with a totally new language—Russian—and a completely foreign alphabet—Cyrillic.

Следующее - российская Кириллица (the following is the Russian Cyrillic alphabet.)

**А Б В Г Д Е Ё Ж Э И К Л
М Н О П Р С Т У Ф Х Ц Ч Ш
Щ Ъ Ы Ь Э Ю Я**

The workload we were under was unrelenting. Every day we were expected to memorize dozens of new words while remembering all those memorized in the previous days, weeks, and months; then add to this a long list of new verb conjugations and a new complicated set of Russian grammar rules. Each night, we committed to memory a four-page story which we had to present in Russian the next day to the rest of the class. We were required to keep up with the daily news from the USSR by reading Russian journals and newspapers. Then, added to all of this was a nightly homework assignment to write a four- to five-page paper on an assigned topic and entirely in Russian.

As the ranking senior officer in our class, it was my responsibility each morning to collect everyone's homework and place it neatly stacked in a pile on Professor Muzenchenko's desk before he walked into the room.

On Friday, the week before graduation, our final homework was due—the last homework assignment that would ever be required of us at the school. The previous evening I had driven from my apartment in Oxon Hill, Maryland, to the Falls Church apartment of classmate and fellow officer, Art Waski, a distance of some 30 miles. Lieutenant Waski was from Minneapolis. He grew up in a Russian family, was fluent in the language, and was the top student in our class.

Like we had done so many times before, he and I studied together in preparation for the following day's class work. Knowing this would be the very last piece of homework I would ever turn in, I wanted a good grade, and I wanted for it to be as perfect as possible.

I arrived at Art's apartment late at night. He read my paper and offered a few suggestions. We then began to work on the rest of our homework for our concluding day of official class work.

At 6:00 AM I drove home. Without any sleep, I showered and shaved, put on my uniform, grabbed my briefcase, and drove to the Naval Station—my final drive to the school as a student. Tired and spent, yet knowing that it would soon all be over, for the very first time in eighteen months, I couldn't wait to get to school.

When I walked into the classroom, like every day of the 500-plus days before, I gathered up everyone's homework and put it in the mandatory, organized, neat pile on Muzenchenko's desk. Hardly believing that in eight hours our ordeal would finally be over, there were hugs, high fives, and loud banter among us. We had made it through!

Precisely at 8:00 AM we stood at attention and waited for Professor Muzenchenko to enter the classroom. While standing there, something started to bother me. I began to question if I had signed my homework. A critical demerit if I hadn't, and one which Muzenchenko would definitely use to lower my grade. I reached for the pile of papers, thumbed through to the last page of my homework, and discovered that, sure enough, my signature was missing. Quickly, I grabbed my pen and wrote my name just as Muzenchenko walked into the room. I placed my homework back on top of the pile and again stood at attention.

Instead of the usual *"Доброе утро, господа"* (Good morning, gentlemen), he said nothing. The room went dead silent.

Knowing he now had me, Muzenchenko looked around the classroom, put his hand on the pile of paperwork, pointed his fat, little, index finger at me and said,

"So, Lieutenant Ramsdell, finally . . . I have caught you cheating."

In that moment it was as if the air had been totally sucked out of the room. No one dared breathe. Standing there at attention, I felt every muscle in my body tighten, ready to explode.

Even my mind seemed paralyzed . . . trying to process what he had just accused me of.

"You are in serious trouble, Lieutenant," he said in his heavy Russian accent. "This will necessitate disciplinary action at the highest level."

Over the years of my life, I've often wondered why I seemed to have been born without a temper. When trying to come up with a reason, I finally decided that, when I was up above, waiting in line with my siblings to get the usual fare of human traits and characteristics that the Good Lord passes out to most of us, my brothers Dick and Ted got confused, took my temper and then shared it equally. I can never remember *ever* totally losing control in my life . . . not until that moment at the Russian Institute.

In a matter of seconds, I leaped over the desk, grabbed Muzenchenko by the throat and threw him to the floor. I ended up on his chest, straddling him, pummeling him with my fists. I was *totally* out of control.

After eighteen months, he had finally broken me. Muzenchenko had won!

Momentarily shocked and stupefied, my classmates quickly recovered and began to pull me off the man who had purposely done everything he could to make our days, weeks, and months at the school a living hell. Oddly, the only words that came babbling from my mouth were Russian swear words. Words too ugly to translate here.

It took all three of my classmates—grown men—to pull me off Muzenchenko, but not before the arrogant, demeaning, miserable, fat little man had his backside kicked. For all the time it took for my classmates to pull me away, I wondered later if they had hesitated on purpose, hoping that I might land a few blows for each one of them.

When my moment of madness ended, the next thing I remembered was being in the administrative headquarters of the school and a jeep of naval MPs (military police) arriving and handcuffing me. Shortly thereafter, I saw Muzenchenko and the director of the Slavic Language Department go into the commandant's office. Ten minutes later, they were joined by my three classmates. I sat on a divan outside the office—an MP on each side. I knew my dream of serving in the military was over. Surely I would be court-martialed and then face charges in a criminal court.

That morning as I had driven to school, I kept thinking to myself,

It's almost over . . . it's almost over.

However, I certainly hadn't expected it to be over like this. Before class, I'd felt a great deal of pride knowing that I'd taken all they could throw at me, and, yet, I had made it through—I was still standing. Twenty-eight bright and gifted students—the best the military had to offer—had started together at the institute. After eighteen months, only four of us were left. Road kill.

Now, sitting on the sofa between the two MPs, a million things went through my head. The one thing my mind wouldn't let go of was how disappointed I was for my dad. Although I was the least favorite of his five sons, I was the only one that had made it into the officer ranks. And now this. I would have a lot of explaining to do, but would he understand . . . or even care?

After an hour, those who had been with the commandant exited his office. As Muzenchenko walked arrogantly in front of my classmates, Lieutenant Waski glanced my way and gave me a nod with a clenched fist down at his side. Ten minutes later, an MP stepped out of the office and my two MP bodyguards escorted me inside. Still handcuffed, I stood at attention in front of the commandant's desk. Commandant O'Shea directed the MPs to remove my handcuffs and asked them to wait outside.

I wanted to rub away the hurt where the tight handcuffs had been, yet, I remained standing at attention. Expecting the worst, but

not having dealt with Commandant O'Shea
before this incident, I was surprised when he
asked me to take a seat.

As the commanding military authority over
the school, Rear Admiral O'Shea was highly
respected in the Washington military circles. A
graduate of the Naval Academy in Annapolis,
he came from a long family line of Naval
officers. It was my understanding that he had
spent the bulk of his career on ships because of
his love of the sea, having grown up in Bar
Harbor, Maine. A tall, thin man with handsome
weathered looks, he proudly wore a chest full
of medals on his dark naval uniform.

He stood up from his chair, slowly walked
around his desk, and then leaned on it close to
where I was sitting. I waited for the hammer to
fall.

"Lieutenant Ramsdell, I know this has been
a tough journey for you and your classmates.
Twenty years ago, I spent a year here at the
institute going through the resident Chinese
program. Only the Good Lord knows the
number of times when I almost lost it and
wanted to quit. Lieutenant," he said, "you've
served here honorably. You've got to be proud
of all you've accomplished in this last year and
a half. I'm aware of the demands you students
are put through here; remember, there were 28

of you when you started. I'm certain I could never do it."

Commandant O'Shea went back to his chair and sat down.

"I want you to take the next ten days off. Go somewhere and clear your mind. I saw from your file that you're married. Take your wife and little boy and go spend some time at the ocean. As someone who grew up on the water, I can tell you that being near the sea is the very best therapy the Lord can provide when we need it most. Don't worry about graduation next week. I'll personally make sure your diploma will be waiting for you when you get back from your time away. What happened here this morning is between you and me and will go no further than this office. Now go gather your things out of your locker and have a great week at the seashore."

Knowing the man could have had me court-martialed, I sat speechless. Not sure how I should respond, I stood at attention, thanked him, and gave him a salute. When he returned my salute, he added,

"Now you owe me a favor, soldier. When I'm finished here at the school next year, my next and final assignment, after twenty-seven years with the military, will be as the Naval Attaché at the American Embassy in Moscow. If you are ever in Moscow during my three-year tour of duty, I expect you to find me and buy me a bowl of that good Russian *borscht* that my Irish *babushka* grandmother used to make when I was a boy. Deal?"

"You've got it, sir," I said. "It's a deal."

Although my heart wanted me to give this larger-than-life man a huge bear hug, protocol would not allow it. Again, I stood at attention, saluted, and walked out of his office . . . a new man.

The following week while at the ocean on the Maryland coast, I sent a carefully worded apology to Professor Muzenchenko. I also sent a postcard to each of my classmates telling them of the good news.

When we returned home to our flat at Oxon Hill, there was a large envelope waiting for me from Commandant O'Shea. Inside the envelope was my diploma and a card. Inside the card were these words.

"Be strong, soldier, and <u>continue</u> to serve proudly."

Chapter 6

A LESSON IN
CHARACTER

*An honest man is the noblest work of
God.*

Alexander Pope

In the spring, shortly after my first wife and
I were married, I graduated from Utah State
University with a degree in political science—
pre-law. That fall I was accepted into law
school at the University of Utah. Two years
later, I had completed half of the requirements
for a law degree. Then, along with dozens of
other graduate students who had been able to
defer their entry date into the military, my
deferment was cancelled and I was called to
active duty.

As a young lieutenant, I spent my first stint in the military as an instructor at the U.S. Intelligence School-Europe, located in Oberammergau, Germany.

For those who have read *A Train to Potevka,* you may recall that the longest chapter in the book details a particular incident I had while performing my staff duty responsibilities at the school. This was when I discovered one of the students, Yuri Novotny, a U.S. Air Force captain, was working for Soviet intelligence.

Despite an occasional setback and other challenges, those early years I spent in the military could not have been more rewarding. I especially enjoyed teaching. And, of course, I loved living in the Alps of southern Germany where the school was located. However, my wife was continually having health problems and wanted to return home to Utah. After I had completed my three-year military obligation, we decided it was best to return to the United States where she could receive better medical care.

Now out of the military and a civilian, I was in need of a job. It was my intention to finish law school part-time while working full-time. During that period, the unemployment rate across the country was exceedingly high. In Utah jobs were scarce.

While reading the want ads in the local newspapers, I learned of a job being offered as a contract administrator in the legal department for a national engineering firm headquartered in Salt Lake City, by the name of Kenway. After competing with about 100 other applicants, I was offered the job. I'm certain the only reason I got the position was the fact that the head of the department, Clyde Christensen, had grown up in my hometown of Bear River and had been a best friend of my older brother Ted.

When Clyde called to inform me that the position would be mine, a heavy burden came off my shoulders. I was so thankful to have a job to support my wife and little boy, especially when the local and national economies were in dire straits.

The morning I reported for work, I met another young man, a recent engineering graduate, also from Utah State University. My new friend, Steve Barlow, was hired on at the firm the very same week as I. My responsibilities were in the contracts department; his responsibilities were in the engineering department.

One of Steve's primary jobs was to prepare the engineering specifications and drawings which would be used as part of a bid package that would be sent out to potential subcontractors when our firm would bid a job as the prime contractor. As a contract specialist, it was my responsibility to add the legal documents to each of these bid packages.

After working for a month or so at Kenway, Steve and I were unexpectedly called into the office of a senior department manager. He explained,

"A new project is being planned by General Motors. Our company is being considered as the prime contractor. We need the very lowest prices from our best subcontractors across the country in order for us to be chosen for this twenty-plus million dollar General Motors job."

Over the next few weeks, Steve and I were responsible for preparing the bid documents and sending them out to specific national subcontractors.

Three weeks passed when we started to receive the bid proposals and pricing back. Once all the subcontractors had responded, we forwarded the pricing information to the Kenway department head. The next morning he summoned both Steve and me to his office.

"You've done a good job," he said, "but, in order to get this General Motors project, we need these subcontractors to lower their bids substantially. If the subcontractors won't, Kenway is not going to be selected as the prime contractor. The pricing we now have is way too high and our company needs this GM job!"

He then took the stack of bid documents and gave half of them to Steve and the other half to me.

"I want you to go back to your offices and call each of the lowest bidders in each category. Tell them they were not the low bidder, and, because we specifically want to use them on the project, they need to cut their pricing by at least a third."

In several instances this meant we were asking some of the subcontractors to reduce their pricing by hundreds of thousands of dollars.

"When you have gathered all the new pricing information," he said, "I want you back in my office this afternoon, no later than four o'clock."

Steve and I grabbed the stacks of documents and left his office. While on the elevator, I told Steve to phone me when he had completed collecting his new pricing information.

"If I finish mine early, I'll come to your office and help you finish your phone calls," I told him.

There was no time for lunch that day; I was too busy making frantic phone calls to subcontractor firms across the country. About 3:00 PM, I had finally collected all the new pricing from the companies as directed by our department head. I contacted Steve and told him I would be right down to help him finish his calls.

When I walked into his office and sat down, I could immediately sense there was a problem.

"Okay," I said. "Where are you with your calls and what can I do to help? Give me some of the files for the companies you haven't contacted. We can have this knocked out in the next half hour or so."

Steve looked at me, slowly shaking his head.

"I haven't made any of the phone calls, Mike. . . . I couldn't do it," he said. "I've spent the last few hours working on a letter of resignation."

His words hit me like a Mack truck. I sat looking down at the floor; struggling for something to say. Here was my friend, a recent college graduate with a wife and three little children. He was willing to resign from his job because he was being asked to do something that he knew was wrong—something that went against his moral compass.

Feeling absolutely worthless, I got up to leave his office. Steve walked me to the door.

"I'm sorry," he said. "I hope this doesn't get you into trouble . . . I just couldn't make those phone calls and misrepresent the truth."

Without saying another word, Steve put his arm around my shoulder and thanked me for my friendship.

"In a few months this will all be forgotten and, hopefully, I'll find a job somewhere else. Mike, no matter what happens," he said, "we need to stay in contact."

Overcome with a mixture of emotions, I didn't—couldn't—speak. I simply nodded my head in the affirmative and left his office.

Back at my desk, I sat in my chair looking at the stack of documents, wondering why I didn't have that kind of integrity. I was ashamed. My friend, with his first full-time job since graduating from college, and knowing how difficult the job market was, was still willing to give up everything in order to keep that which, to him, was most important—his personal honor and integrity as a human being.

For weeks after this experience, perhaps even months after, not a day went by when I didn't think about Steve and the lesson he had taught me. From that day forward, I promised myself I would pay more attention to the qualities of integrity and honor and work to make them an integral part of my own life. Like Steve, I wanted to be able to face whatever challenges and difficulties came my way knowing I had done the right thing. Most of us, of course, never measure up to be the person we want to be or know we should be. There is comfort, however, in the knowledge that, while living each day, we can at least try.

And now the rest of the story . . .

A few years later when Kenway was bought by Eaton Corporation, a Fortune 500 Company out of Cleveland, Ohio, the new owners totally reorganized their new acquisition. Part of this reorganization, which is often the case when a corporate takeover happens, was to streamline and downsize most of the departments. With little seniority in the company, I was the first person let go from the contracts department. However, during the downsizing of the engineering department, a certain young engineer was able to keep his job. Years later, this same engineer was named Senior Vice President and Director of Sales and Marketing of Eaton-Kenway . . . my good friend—Steve Barlow.

Chapter 7

HEALING THE HEART

There's a destiny that makes us brothers.
None goes his way alone.
All that we send into the lives of others,
Will come back into our own

Edwin Markham

A few years ago, when my book, *A Train to Potevka*, was at its peak in popularity, the requests for me to speak were also at an all-time high.

After one of my speaking engagements, I was approached by a woman who had been in the audience. She explained she was a booking agent working with a national speakers bureau. She represented Mike Schlappi, one of the most popular and successful motivational speakers in the country; she handled all of his speaking engagements. The following day she and I met for lunch. Based upon what she had observed the night before at my presentation, she proposed that she sign me on as one of her clients.

Not knowing who Mike Schlappi was, while together at lunch, I sat spellbound as she told me the remarkable story of this man's life, and how, as a young athlete, he had been involved in a tragic accident which left him a paraplegic.

As a young teenager, Schlappi was a gifted athlete. The morning of his school's championship football game, he stopped by a teammate's home. After knocking on the door, he heard his friend's voice telling him to come in. Mike followed the sound of the voice to the master bedroom. While waiting for his friend to come out of the bathroom, Mike noticed a handgun sitting on a chest of drawers. When the teammate came out of the bathroom, his friend picked up the gun, thinking it was unloaded, and pulled it from the holster. Mike sat on the bed and watched. Without any bad intentions, his friend lowered the gun, pointed it at Mike in jest, and pulled the trigger. Bam! The bullet hit Mike in the chest, punctured his right lung, and severed his spinal cord.

In a panic and not able to breathe or stand, Mike remembers promising God that if He would let him live, he would devote his life to becoming a better person.

In telling his incredible story to audiences, Mike relates how he was able to forgive his friend and deal with the challenges he had to face. It was due to his mother and father's love and encouragement that he realized he could still be a great athlete and a contributing member of society.

After endless months of physical therapy, he began to regain his strength and acquire new skills. Within a year he was competing in wheelchair marathons. Mike Schlappi went on to become one of the most decorated wheelchair athletes ever. He played on eleven international teams and won medals at three different Olympics. His remarkable message is that adversity and challenges can make one a better person. Mike is married with a beautiful wife and large family. He now travels the country as a highly successful motivational speaker. Mike Schlappi is truly a living American hero.

Mike Ramsdell

(Note: You can order Mike Schlappi's book or DVD or schedule a speaking event at www.mikeschlappi.com.)

During my meeting with Mike Schlappi's agent, she gave me a DVD of one of his presentations. I took the DVD home that evening and watched it several times before retiring. I was astonished to see what Mike Schlappi had survived and, as a paraplegic, what he has been able to accomplish with his life.

The following day, a week before Christmas, I put the DVD in my briefcase as I prepared to leave for four days of Costco book signings in Twin Falls, Nampa, and Boise, Idaho. During those days in Idaho, I had book signings during the day and speaking engagements on all three of the evenings.

When I finished my final book signing at the Boise Costco, I drove to nearby Caldwell, where I spoke to a large group at a retired seniors facility. Although it was already late when I left the speaking engagement and beginning to snow, it was my intention to drive home the 350 miles straight through to where my wife and I live in Davis County, Utah. I was anxious to get home to Bonnie and help her with the final preparations for Christmas—our favorite time of the year.

Only an hour out of Boise and with the snow getting worse, I knew my tired body was not going to be able to make the five-hour drive. I made a phone call to Bonnie and she agreed that I should not try to travel at such a late hour, but, instead, get a motel and rest up for the drive in the morning.

While trying to decide in which town I should get a room for the night, I remembered that Mountain Home Air Force Base was a short drive west, just off the freeway.

While going through security at the main gate, I was given directions to the officers' lodging facility by the military police. It was only a few days before Christmas, but, still, I was surprised that the parking lot was empty with the exception of two cars. Had the entire base gone home for the holidays? I grabbed my luggage from my vehicle and walked into the building.

As I approached the front desk, I was greeted by two female airmen. The plump one with the chubby cheeks and wild hair was the most talkative of the two. The quiet, attractive one looked like she had been a college athlete in her younger years and was still determined to keep her hourglass figure. They were both cordial and helpful. Abby, the heavyset one joked,

"Good news, sir. Seeing as you're our only customer tonight, you have the entire facility to yourself."

Rather than put me in a standard officer's room, they were kind enough to give me a VIP suite. I thanked them both. Not knowing if I would see them again in the morning, I wished them both a Merry Christmas.

I grabbed my bag and briefcase and walked down the hallway to my room. Once inside, I unpacked a few essentials and then turned my attention to the television console and DVD player. From my briefcase I pulled out the Schlappi DVD. Although I had thought about it numerous times during my four days away from home, due to my nonstop schedule of book signings and speaking events, I hadn't had time to watch the DVD again.

After ten frustrating minutes of trying to get the DVD player to work, I finally gave up and walked back down the hallway to the front desk.

Although reluctant, it was my intention to ask the chunky airman to return to my room with me to help me resolve the problem with the DVD player. As luck would have it, however, when I got to the front desk there sat the beautiful airman.

"Can I help you, sir?" she asked.

"Yes," I replied. "When your coworker comes back could you ask her to please come to my room. I'm having trouble getting the DVD player to work."

"Sir," she said, "Abby has gone to dinner and will not be back for an hour. I'd be happy to help you. Besides with you as our only customer, it has been really slow around here."

"I'm sorry to be a bother," I said. "I know it doesn't sound like a big thing, but getting the DVD player to work would be appreciated."

She introduced herself as Airman Carol Herrera, and together we walked down the hallway to my room. I was feeling uncomfortable and wondered if she was thinking I had questionable motives behind my request.

When we got to my room, I unlocked the door and swung it wide open. I used my briefcase as a doorstop so the door would remain open out into the hallway. Once inside, Airman Herrera grabbed the nearest chair and placed herself in front of the TV. After approximately three minutes the Schlappi DVD was up and running. She stood up from the chair, but her eyes remained riveted on the screen as Mike Schlappi gave his presentation in front of a large audience while moving around the stage in his wheelchair.

Still uncomfortable with her there in my room, I thanked her for her help expecting she would now leave. However, she did not move; her eyes were glued to the television screen.

I started to explain about Mike Schlappi and the DVD, but she put her index finger to her lips in a gesture meaning that she wanted to hear what was being said. As the DVD played, I couldn't help but notice how emotional she became. From the nightstand I handed her a small box of Kleenex. While continually wiping away tears, she clutched a wet ball of Kleenex, squeezing it with her fists, moving it from one hand to the other, all the while saying, "He's got to see this. He's got to see this. He's got to see this."

Unable to understand her behavior, I was concerned about how emotional and distraught she had become. After fifteen minutes, I was relieved when the DVD finally ended. Wiping her eyes and trying to fix her smeared makeup, she turned to me to apologize. Her words came very painfully.

"Colonel Ramsdell," she said, "three weeks ago my nineteen year old son fell nine stories from the top of an oil rig in the Gulf of Mexico. Billy lost both of his legs." She paused, not able to continue for a moment.

"I've just come back from spending the last two weeks with him at the Memorial Hospital in Houston. My husband is still there with him."

"Sir," she said, "I don't know the circumstances that brought you here tonight, but I know you were supposed to come here and we were supposed to meet. Without his legs, my Billy doesn't want to live anymore. No matter how we, the doctors, nurses, and therapists try to encourage him, he doesn't want to go on living. He's convinced that, as a paraplegic, he will only be a burden to everyone around him; and his life will be meaningless.

"The coincidences of you getting a room here tonight, the problems with the DVD player, and the chance for me to see and hear how Mr. Schlappi has been able to overcome his challenges and disabilities is a miracle for our family. Seeing this DVD tonight is the first time in the last three weeks that I've had any hope. My son needs to see this. Once my husband and I can watch this DVD with Billy, I just know it will be the thing to turn him around and make him realize that he can still have a full, productive, and meaningful life."

Back at the front desk, we exchanged contact information; addresses, phone numbers, and emails. I promised Carol that before doing anything else, my number one priority when I got home in the morning would be to secure a copy of the Schlappi DVD and send it to her by Federal Express.

We talked for another thirty minutes or more until her coworker returned from dinner. Miss Talkative sat silently as Carol told her what had taken place while Abby had been at dinner. Again, Airman Herrera could not hold her emotions while retelling her son's story and the coincidence of me and the Mike Schlappi DVD. Yet the entire time, through the tears, she had a definite smile of hope on her face.

I thanked them again, wished them a Merry Christmas, and headed for my room. I got into bed exhausted. Yet, sleep would not come. I thought of Mike Schlappi: his heroism, his attitude, perseverance and, despite his challenges, all the incredible things he has been able to accomplish in his life. I kept rolling over in my mind the coincidences of the decision to get a room at the air force base, the problems with the DVD player, and Airman Herrera working on that particular nightshift as the front desk clerk. I thought how, to some, He is not a God of miracles anymore. But as for me and Carol, we would argue otherwise.

Two nights before Christmas, at an empty officers' quarters at Mountain Home AFB in Idaho, I was blessed to be a messenger, a bearer of "Good Tidings" at Christmas time: a witness to the care and concern of a loving Heavenly

Father. I thought about Billy, lying in a hospital bed in Houston, Texas—the struggles and challenges he had ahead of him—and how much his family loved him.

And, as Tiny Tim exclaimed, from Charles Dickens' *A Christmas Carol* . . . God Bless Us Every One!

Thank you, Lord, for this blessing of being a messenger; and thank you, Mike Schlappi.

STARTING POINTS

FROM RUSSIA WITH LOVE

POTEVKA'S BEGINNINGS

Chapter 8

FROM RUSSIA WITH LOVE

Dare to be great as God meant for you to be!

Max B. Richardson

I'm often asked how a country boy from a small town like Bear River could possibly end up working in the spy world in Russia. It all happened because of my dad—Dewey is to blame.

My dad was a true patriot. He was not a religious man per se; his religion was how much he loved this country. At age 13 my dad quit school to work on the railroad in the mines of Park City. During World War I, Dad misrepresented his age and served in the military until the war's end. When he returned home, Dad met my mom; eventually they were married and began to raise a large family. Mom and Dad had three beautiful daughters and five sons. Four of those sons—a little humor here—were quite homely. My brothers were born almost one after another and then, a dozen years later, this mistake came along—me. As we grew up, Dad would often remind us, especially his sons, how fortunate we were to be born in America with all its opportunities and freedoms.

When my older brothers reached adulthood and were eligible to join the military, that's what they did. I'm certain Dad's patriotism and love of country had a great deal to do with their decisions to serve. Because of the age disparity between me and my brothers, I was still a boy when they joined the armed forces. Wanting to also honor our dad and my brothers, even at a very young age I, too, knew that someday I would be part of the military. The more I learned, however, about the various branches of the armed forces, the more I was determined not to be just an ordinary soldier. My dream was to someday fly jets as an Air Force pilot.

In the summers, while working in the fields of Bear River planting, hoeing, and harvesting for the local farmers, I would often see fighter jets overhead. When hearing their muted roar, I would stop whatever I was doing and look skyward. Almost every afternoon you could see planes from Hill Air Force Base flying high above the Bear River Valley on their training missions. Watching them do their aerial maneuvers was fascinating to me. That was when I would promise myself,

"Mike, that's how you're going to serve your country someday; you are going to be an Air Force pilot."

Upon graduation from Utah State University, I was accepted into law school at the University of Utah. I was halfway through law school when those of us who had already been commissioned as military officers through the university ROTC program had our deferments cancelled and were called to active duty.

At the time the military had a special program that allowed a person to apply directly to flight school if one already had their undergraduate degree. Of course, there had to be a significant exchange of information: transcripts of credits, security clearance verification, health records, and the like. Knowing there would be a great deal of competition to get accepted into the program, we were told that the first week would be a probationary period.

Along with 99 other college graduates, I was sent to an air base outside of Denver, Colorado.

111

The first week, which they called test week—we called it wash out week—we were put through every problematic situation imaginable to determine if we had the so-called "Right Stuff." They tested our physical abilities, mental capacities, and psyches. They did this in order to find out if a country boy like me had what it takes to learn to fly one of their $15 million jets.

On Wednesday of that maddening week, my roommate suggested, "Mike, let's take a break from all this craziness and go into Denver tonight and see the hot movie of the summer."

I had heard about the movie and the main actor but had seen neither.

"I agree," I told him, "we definitely need a break from all of this."

That night we sat in a movie theater in downtown Denver, Colorado, and there on the silver screen—and this will date me—we saw a movie entitled "From Russia with Love." It was the second James Bond 007 movie ever filmed.

Not growing up with books in our home, and with my family not owning a television until my mid-teens, I'd had very little exposure to the world of spies and clandestine work. Like it happened yesterday, I still remember sitting in my seat that night totally mesmerized by what I saw: all the suspense and intrigue, the spy paraphernalia, the fast cars, the faster jets, and, of course, the beautiful 007 women. And—again, a little humor here—I couldn't believe how much I looked like Sean Connery.

As the movie was ending, I leaned over and told my roommate, "That's how I want to serve this country . . . I want to work in the spy world."

By week's end I had arranged to be administratively released from the flight program; a few months later my career started in military intelligence.

By no means was I at the top of any of my classes academically, so how is it that I was accepted into the Intelligence Corps?

A few years earlier I had taken a break from my university studies to serve a church mission in Europe. Half of my mission was served in Germany; so I spoke German. The other half of my mission I served in Switzerland and, therefore, spoke Swietzerdeutsch. The other foreign language that I was fluent in—and still remain fluent in today—is that language we speak in my hometown of "Bar" River. It was my foreign language abilities that opened the door. And that's how my career began in military intelligence.

After completing officers' basic training, I got orders to attend the U.S. Intelligence Command and School in Ft. Huachuca in southern Arizona just outside of Sierra Vista and not far from the US/Mexican border. We simply referred to the place as "spook school."

I was fascinated by the course work. I couldn't believe all that there was to learn about the intelligence world and being an agent. The spook school cadre kept us busy from early morning until late each night with not only compelling classroom instruction, but, also, with a lot of practical field work.

After spending a demanding year at the school as a student, I graduated with my credentials as a counterintelligence agent.

At the time of graduation, many of us who were considering a career in intelligence were given the opportunity to fill out a wish list of the countries in which we wanted to specialize.

Growing up at the height of the Cold War, I had always been intrigued with Russia, the other world superpower. As a boy I remember many times sitting on the floor in front of our family's big Philco console radio while my dad tuned in a nightly newscast by Edward R. Murrow. To my young mind, each broadcast seemed the same: in a few days the great Russian Bear was going to unleash its wrath, invade the United States, and eat all our children. When speaking to youth groups today, I'm surprised at how few young people even know of, or understand, what it was like growing up during the Cold War.

Now a full-fledged counterintelligence agent and ready to go out and conquer the world, I wrote at the top of my wish list . . . Russia. I don't remember my second or third choice, because after only a few weeks I was notified that I had been accepted into the Russian program.

However, fear and trembling came upon my body when I received orders to report to the Russian Institute in Washington D.C. where I would spend the next year and a half getting the equivalent of a master's degree in Russian Studies and the Russian language.

Why fear and trembling? Because, during my years in school, I had never seriously applied myself academically. My priorities had been: my best friends, girls, football, girls, sports, and girls. As far as I was concerned, I'd had my priorities in the right place. Now, however, being a student at the Russian Institute, there was no way I dared fail. If I did not graduate, certainly, my military career would, for all intents and purposes, be over.

When sometimes relating this story to audiences—to add a little levity—I ask them to please applaud at the appropriate moment. Then I go on to tell them that after a year and half, this Bear River farm boy graduated from the Russian Institute fourth in his class. And if I'm not speaking in a chapel, the audience will usually work with me and respond with loud applause.

When the applause ends, I pick out someone near the front row who didn't seem all that impressed that I graduated fourth in my class.

"Have you got a problem?" I will ask, which of course makes the person and the audience uncomfortable. Then, looking disgusted and shaking my head, I turn to the audience and announce,

"This gentleman wants to know how many students were in my class." This, too, always gets a big laugh. Then I work the moment, telling the audience,

"There always has to be at least one of his type in the crowd." Finally, I look directly at my supposed accuser and tell him,

"Okay, okay . . . there were four in my class." This, again, really gets the audience going. But it is actually true.

In contrast to how much I enjoyed my year at spook school, the year and a half at the Russian Institute, however, was quite a different story.

All of our professors were native Russians. The faculty had a reputation of being demanding, unreasonable, and absolutely not interested in excuses. You towed the line academically or you were gone!

The work load we carried as students was overwhelming. In truth, I probably lived on a maximum of four to five hours of sleep each night during my time at the institute. Opening day we started with twenty-eight students; only four of us graduated.

After graduation, I was given a few weeks of furlough before my first assignment. When I had been back home in Bear River for about two weeks, my orders came in the mail. For my very first military assignment, I was selected to be an instructor of Soviet/Russian studies at the U.S. Intelligence School-Europe located in Oberammergau, Germany. I was ecstatic!

Two weeks later my wife, little boy, and I flew in late January from Salt Lake International to JFK in New York and then on to Frankfurt, Germany. At the Frankfurt Hauptbahnhof (main train station), we took a train to Garmisch-Partinkirchen, a ski resort town nestled in the Alps on the border between Germany and Austria. After the five-hour train trip, there, waiting for us at the Garmisch Train Station, was the entire cadre of instructors from the intelligence school. These were the men and women with whom I would be teaching for the next three years.

Located in the beautiful German Alps, Garmisch, Oberammergau, and the surrounding area has to be one of the most beautiful, picturesque, places in all the world. That evening, after a faculty-welcoming dinner of Wiener Schnitzel, sauerkraut—oh, how I love German food—and oompah band music, we drove up the winding mountain road from Garmisch to Oberammergau where the intelligence school campus was located. A moonlit night, mountains covered deep with snow; the scenery was absolutely breathtaking.

After almost three non-stop years of schooling, I was finally beginning my first assignment as a counterintelligence agent. I thought back on all that had taken place in the years since leaving Bear River. To be in Europe as an instructor at the U.S. Intelligence School, in one of the most beautiful places in the world—the German Alps—I felt I had died and gone to heaven. How could it ever get any better than this?

Chapter *9*

POTEVKA'S BEGINNINGS

Keep away from people who try to belittle your ambitions. Small people always do that, but the really great make you feel that you, too, can become great.

Mark Twain

When responding to the often-asked question as to how my book, *A Train to Potevka,* came to be, the response is one of my favorite stories to share with others.

Without a doubt, I am one of the most unlikely people to ever write a book. Yet, against so many odds and so many naysayers, the book went on to become a best seller. The experience of writing *Potevka* has blessed the lives of Bonnie and me more than we could have ever imagined.

And how did it all happen . . .?

Having been a wannabe athlete most of my life, and after playing team sports through my high school and college years, it was my goal to continue to enjoy sports by remaining physically active throughout my life.

This is when I first fell in love with the individual sports of racquetball, tennis, and skiing. Although I did not come to racquetball until several years after college, I immediately took to the sport. I love its demands of speed, hand-eye coordination, agility, and endurance. One hour of competitive racquetball, in my opinion, is equal to two or three hours on the tennis court.

I was introduced to racquetball only a year or so before I accepted the assignment to live and work in Russia for several years. In a country of over 300 million people, how many racquetball courts do they have? One. At the American Embassy in Moscow. However, because of my responsibilities working in intelligence there, I had little opportunity to use the gymnasium amenities at the embassy. During those years abroad, I definitely missed the game of racquetball.

When my assignment in Russia was finally done, it was time for me to retire and return home to America. Bonnie and I left Moscow and flew to Washington, D.C. where I said goodbye to my colleagues. Two days later we flew to Salt Lake City. From there, we were driven to Hill Air Force Base where we stayed at the officers' quarters for a month while locating an apartment where we would live during the construction of our home.

On our second day back home at Hill Air Force Base, I drove to a nearby storage unit in Kaysville where all our household goods had been stored during our years in Russia. It took me over an hour, but I finally found my racquetball bag and gear. The next day I was back on the courts trying to remember which end of the racquet to hold. It had been a long, long time.

After all I had gone through and all the close calls I had faced during my time in Russia, I was grateful to be in one piece. When Bonnie and I lived in Moscow during the calamity of the fall of the Soviet Empire, it was considered the most dangerous city in the world. That was now all behind me; I was finally home. Bonnie and I had all my retirement years ahead of us. We had grand plans: build our dream home, travel, take classes together at the university, and most important . . . spend time with grandkids that were coming into the family.

Only home a few weeks from Russia, I was on the racquetball court running flat out for a shot when one sneaker stepped on the other. I tripped and catapulted head first into the front wall. When I regained consciousness, I saw multiple psychedelic images on the ceiling above.

How could this be? What had happened? I mumbled. *It's absolutely forbidden for an agent to do drugs. So, . . .?*

I was taken to a nearby medical facility where emergency room doctors assured me that my injury was nothing to be concerned about. After explaining to the ER physician the details of how the accident had happened—slamming head first into a wall—he still chose not to take x-rays. He assured me, again, that I would be okay and sent me home.

After a week of my condition continually getting worse—I was having problems with numbness in my arms and hands—I made an appointment to be seen by doctors from the University of Utah Medical Center. After I told them how the accident happened, the first thing they did was order x-rays. After reading them, they came to my room and gave me the bad news,

"Mr. Ramsdell, you have fractured your neck."

Words cannot express how angry I was. After all my dangerous years in Russia, I had returned home to fracture my neck while playing racquetball.

During the first few weeks after the accident, I was so mad at the world, the Lord, at Bonnie, and, even at her three cats (Gorbachev, Yeltsin, and Putin). I'd rather have been wounded in a gun battle with the KGB on the streets of downtown Moscow.

As the endless days of physical therapy began, Bonnie could see how discouraged I was getting. Definitely, I was not someone you wanted to be around. Wisely, even her cats kept their distance.

After six-weeks passed, I was still depressed and feeling sorry for myself. One day Bonnie came into the bedroom with our laptop computer.

"Why don't you consider using your recovery time to write a short story for your grandkids about your time in Russia?"

"Don't bother me," I snapped. "I know what you're trying to do."

My first reaction was to throw the laptop across the room. Me . . . write? I was in no mood to even consider such a proposition. Mainly, however, because I had never written. In fact, during my senior year in high school at Bear River, I was the student usually asked to leave Mr. Morris' English class and report to Principal Kerr's office. Why did I have to pay attention during class? Besides, I already spoke English just fine, thank you.

Simply put, I was an average student in school, doing just enough to get by. My quarterly report card included the occasional 'A' but, admittedly, those were for athletics, student council, and a cappella choir. I was too busy hanging out with my best friends, playing sports, and dating those beautiful Bear River High coeds. I never applied myself academically, which I still regret to this day. Of all the mandatory classes I had to take, English—writing and reading and learning about great literature—was the one class I was least fond of. And more than anything, I had no interest in creative writing. Even while in the military and during my assignments with the intelligence services, I would usually have one of my staff people write my reports.

However, Bonnie's challenge kept rolling around in my head. For a couple of days I stared at the laptop near my bed. Finally, having nothing else to do, I decided I could at least give it a try.

I spent the first few hours making a list of possible things I could write about. And then, as I began to write in earnest, the magic happened; the memories and emotions of my years working in Russia and Scandinavia came flooding back. Because of the numbness in my hands and arms, I could only use my two index fingers to poke at the keyboard; but soon the words started to appear. After only a couple of hours, I had created a list of some of the experiences that I'd had during my years abroad.

The initial story, which started out for my grandkids, began turning into something more; something that, perhaps, even grownups might enjoy reading. Surprisingly, and totally unexpectedly, a strange thing began to happen; I was actually enjoying putting my words down on paper. Mr. Morris . . .where are you?

Knowing that Christmas was soon approaching, I decided to write about an experience that involved Russia, a safe house, a package, and my sister Karen. My ten–page, short story would be a Christmas gift to her.

Only when I got the story completely done would I let Bonnie read it. She was definitely surprised and impressed: not with how well the story was written but with the fact that her husband knew where to place the periods.

"Mike, your writing isn't that bad," she said. "I think this is good enough that we should send it to our family and friends as a Christmas gift."

To say the least, her comments pleased me. But then again, was her praise due to her being a supportive wife or did she really mean it?

I worked the next week to fine tune the story while Bonnie added the proper punctuation. We had Kinko's print fifty copies and, as Bonnie suggested, we sent them out to family and friends as Christmas gifts.

After the holidays we began to receive emails and phone calls thanking us for the ten-page story, including several encouraging remarks that I should consider putting other possible stories together in a book.

Even before such positive feedback, I was had begun to enjoy the whole writing process; for me, it was very cathartic. After that first month, I concluded, *Mike, you can do this after all.*

Therefore, I took a leap of faith and decided to put my stories together as a book. I spent the rest of the winter and spring writing. As I continued to write, each day more experiences came back from my past. It never once, however, crossed my mind that someday my writing would evolve into a book that people would want to purchase.

During the first six months, I probably spent two to three hours every other night writing. With no pressure, no time schedule, and no publisher breathing down my neck, my first experience with writing couldn't have been more enjoyable. I wasn't trying to prove anything to anyone. I just enjoyed the challenge of putting the stories together and making them readable.

At the beginning of the summer, after I had written about half of the manuscript, I was confronted by one of my brothers for being so stupid that I would waste my time writing a book.

"Who do you think you are that anyone would want to read what you have to say? What a waste of time," he said scornfully.

His words cut deeply. In truth, in spite of the many positive responses I'd received, I still had doubts and misgivings. My brother's comments took the air out of me like a kick in the stomach, and they festered. I didn't write for the next several days, and I finally came to the conclusion that he was right. Who was I to think that *anyone* would care about what I had to say? I gathered up my notes and the two hundred pages of manuscript and put them in the garbage.

It's amazing the power and influence an older sibling can have.

Bonnie and I never discussed the confrontation with my brother. I spent the summer staying busy working on projects around the house and doing the landscaping for our new home. The highlight of the summer was a trip Bonnie and I made to the East Coast where we spent two weeks back in one of our favorite cities, Washington, D.C.

A few days after we returned home, Bonnie came to me with a file box. In it were all of the *Potevka* papers and notes which I had thrown away.

"OK, cowboy," she said, "it's time to get back to work. Remember what your high school football coach taught you. You don't quit! You have an obligation to yourself to finish the book. And I want you to finish it, not for me or anyone else, but for yourself."

Those were words I needed to hear.

The next day I was at my desk totally immersed in my writing. I probably wrote two hours a night, every night, until the manuscript was finally completed six months later.

Once it was finished, we tried to find a printer in the Salt Lake/Ogden area who would print a dozen copies. No printer would entertain the idea. Using the Internet, Bonnie, fortunately, located a printer in Tennessee who agreed to print their minimum run—one hundred copies. We sent the manuscript to the printer along with a check. Six weeks later a UPS truck unloaded a pallet containing five boxes with twenty books in each box.

Like it was yesterday, I will always remember the moment when I used my Swiss Army knife to cut away the cellophane wrap covering the pallet. I picked up the box nearest me, cut the top open with my knife, reached in and pulled out a copy of my book. Wow!

For those who have written and for those who will someday write, what a moment! I held in my hands the stories of my years as an intelligence officer in Russia, Europe, and Scandinavia, including a few of my experiences as a father, a friend, and a brother. I was absolutely thrilled.

With book in hand, I walked from the garage up the back steps to the kitchen. Bonnie was there finishing the dishes. I held the book up, moving it from side to side with a big "look what I've got" grin on my face.

"Do you have anything to say to me for the next five hours?" I asked.

Bonnie, in her inimitable way, walked up and put her arms around me.

"Mike," she said. "I'm so proud of you for sticking with it and seeing it through. Look at what you've accomplished! No one can ever take that away from you."

At that moment I was as high as a kite. I walked upstairs to our den, opened the book and began to read. Five hours later I finished, closed the cover, and thought to myself,

Wow . . . I want to meet this guy!

Like I have encouraged others during my presentations, when you write your book or record your life's experiences, you'll be amazed by what a story it will tell. I truly believe there is a book in each one of us, and what a treasure that book will be to your family and friends. And, you never know, perhaps, even Oprah might call.

From those 100 books, we probably gave away more than half of them to family and friends. After less than a month, we started receiving phone calls asking where the book could be purchased.

"You can't buy it. It's not for sale anywhere," I would tell people.

"Mike, just for the heck of it, why don't we take a dozen books up to Tremonton and ask Feldman's Bookstore to sell them on consignment?" Bonnie suggested. (Bonnie has always been the smart one of this partnership.) A few days later, I drove the sixty miles to Tremonton and I met with Mrs. Feldman. She agreed to take the books but advised me,

"Please be back in a week or so to pick them up."

A few days later Mrs. Feldman called to tell me that she was out of books. Not only that, she wanted me to consider doing a book signing at her bookstore. To say I was thrilled is an understatement. Later, we took more books to Tremonton and made a similar arrangement with a bookstore in Brigham City and one in Logan.

Then came the "mother of all phone calls," which went something like this:

"Mr. Ramsdell," the person on the other end of the phone asked, "are you the one who wrote *A Train to Potevka*?"

"Yes," I answered.

"And how many books do you have?"

I looked at the books stacked on the floor near the corner of my desk.

"Nine," I replied.

"How soon could we get a few thousand copies?" (This eventually lead to initial orders of 35,000 books over the next few weeks.)

"Who is this?" I asked, somewhat irritated. I was sure I was being set up by one of my friends.

"Mr. Ramsdell, this is Costco."

And my reply . . . "What's a Costco?"

I probably had heard of them, but I really didn't know who they were. The parents of a local Costco manager had read one of those first one hundred books and encouraged their son that his local Costco warehouse should carry it.

Once I realized the magnitude of what that phone call could eventually mean, I was on cloud nine. I ordered a reprint of the books, and a few weeks later did my first Costco signing in Ogden, Utah. As book sales began to grow, it wasn't long before I was traveling around the West doing book signings at Costcos throughout Utah, Idaho, Colorado, Nevada, Arizona, California, Oregon, and Washington.

After working during the last few years exclusively with Costco managers and staff, I can say without reservation, they are the most professional corporation I have ever dealt with. I am honored to have the opportunity to be associated with such a great company and great people.

These last few years since I wrote *Potevka* have been an amazing ride. Most mornings, I wake up and pinch myself that all this has happened. Yet I often think of my brothers and the other naysayers who, for whatever reason, were so negative about my book. Especially when one considers that: *A Train to Potevka* eventually became a best seller; an estimated million-plus people have now read the book; I've had the opportunity to speak about the book and my career at hundreds of venues around the country; I lecture on cruise ships around the world; and, although moving slowly, the *Potevka* movie is moving forward . . . it is going to happen.

All of this begs the question . . . who fractured my neck? Perhaps part of the answer lies in what I wrote five years ago regarding my experiences in the village of Potevka:

> *It is not the Lord's way or His plan to take away our hardships and difficulties. It is these challenges that give us the opportunity to grow in faith, character, and understanding. And if we won't give up, He will be at our side to help us see them through.*

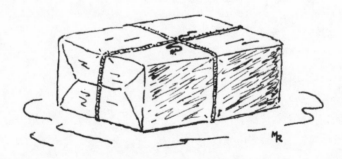

FIVE YEARS AND COUNTING

COSTCO CHARACTERS

BOOK CLUBS AND JELL-O

KEYNOTES AND FIRESIDES

CLANDESTINE Q&A

EPILOGUE

Chapter 10

COSTCO CHARACTERS

*We are all fellow passengers on the same
planet.*

Hendrick van Loon

I was recently told that my book, *A Train to
Potevka*, has been selling at various Costcos in
the Western states, with a few breaks now and
again, for five years. Considering that most
books have a shelf life in Costco of three
months, this news made me both grateful and
very proud.

Working with Costco has been one of the
most rewarding and enjoyable experiences I
have had. Their corporate philosophy of
providing a quality product at a fair price has
made them one of the most successful

companies in America. When the business world comes out with their annual publications of the five or ten best companies in America to work for, Costco is always included on such lists. I have had the opportunity to personally get to know many of their managers and found them to be, in every way, exceptional people. These managers and their staff oversee 350 workers at their facility and have sales of hundreds of thousands of dollars each day.

Without Costco, my book would never have had the success it has. I was the only self-published, local author to do book signings for the first two years after my book was released. Then, as in most successful ventures, other local publishers began having their authors follow suit with signings at Costco. Many of these authors have had significant success. However, to be the first self-published author to do signings with Costco gives me a great deal of pride.

As you might have heard, in recent years the publishing industry has been turned on its head. For an author, there is no more need to spend years trying to get a book accepted by an agent and then by a national publisher. With the advent of printing-on-demand, any author can self publish and do the marketing themselves.

I have to admit, I was very fortunate to be picked up by Costco just after I wrote *A Train to Potevka.* Although I've had invitations to market and do book signings with other national chains, my loyalty is to Costco. They were the ones who first believed in me and my book, and I hope my relationship with them will continue for many more years and many more books.

If I had to point to one event that seemed to make all the difference with the success of my book, it would be when, a few years ago, Costco chose to do a full-page article about my book for the *Author Spotlight* in the Christmas issue of their monthly corporate magazine, *The Costco Connection.* This magazine is mailed to millions of Costco members. That article brought national attention to *A Train to Potevka,* and it was upwards and onwards from there.

In these five years of book signings, I've had so many experiences: some good, some bad, some strange, and, unfortunately, some sad. The majority of the signings I have done have been in the Western states.

People often ask me if I get tired of doing Costco book signings and eating those famous Costco hotdogs for lunch. Nothing could be further from the truth. I'm proud of my book and its message, and I love the opportunity to visit with old friends, make new friends, and work with the great Costco managers and staff.

However, I do laugh when I think of some of the characters I've seen in the various Costcos who make their noon rounds everyday for the free samples. It seems each Costco store has the same twenty men and women who are there every single day; some I've gotten to know personally. I teasingly chide them that Costco is soon going to make them pay a "grazing fee." However, I'm certainly not without guilt. Whenever a book signing is too busy for me to grab a Costco hot dog or slice of pizza, a quick trip to the food vendors has quieted my empty stomach on many occasions.

As the following stories relate, there are interactions with the shopping public that seem to happen at these Costco signings on a regular basis:

THE RUSSIAN EXPERT

One or two times a week, I'm confronted by someone who has recently traveled to Russia or visited the former Soviet Union years ago. For whatever reason, that person will stay at my table for hours telling me every minute detail of their trip: the hotels where they slept, the restaurants where they ate, the museums and art galleries they visited, and every Russian person they came in contact with. Although I personally lived and worked in Russia for years and years, I get a kick out of the fact that these well-meaning people still want to enlighten me about everything Russia: Putin, politics, the economy, the mafia, government, foreign policy, etc., etc.

ГОВОРИТ КАК УРОЖЕНЕЦ
SPEAKS LIKE A NATIVE

Another common experience is with those who have sons or daughters that are serving, or have served, as church missionaries in one of the missions in Russia. Often, they tell me their missionary has become so fluent in the language that most Russians think he or she is native.

Understanding how proud they are, I never contradict them or burst their bubble. In reality, however, other than for a few standard phrases, most Russian linguists would have a hard time believing this could be true. Russian is a very difficult language. I have spoken Russian for many years and still struggle with verb conjugations and correct grammatical endings. Even considering all the correct grammar required when speaking, it is almost impossible to truly master the unique idiomatic, expressions in the language. During my years as a German missionary, I was fluent and comfortable when speaking about religion. However, when other subjects came up such as the economy, business, or foreign policy, like most other missionaries, I was usually lost.

REMEMBER ME?

One of the fun things that happens is when someone will come to my book signing table and ask,

"Mike, do you remember me?"

They forget or don't realize that, since my book came out, including all the speaking engagements and book signings I've done around the country, I have probably met over a quarter of a million people. After an obviously confused and puzzled look crosses my face, accompanied by a slow nod of my head, they follow up with something like,

"Surely you remember; we met at the Costco in Wilsonville, Oregon. I think it was two years ago."

Not wanting to be impolite, I usually try to reply with a comment similar to, "Maybe . . . so. I think it's coming back to me now."

Meeting such interesting, sometimes different, but wonderful people has helped to make my weeks, months, and years of Costco signings truly memorable.

RUSSIAN MAIL-ORDER BRIDES

One of the sad things that happens now and again is when a gentleman will come by my table, seemingly just to visit. However, after five or ten minutes of small talk and becoming acquainted, he finally asks my opinion about Russian mail-order brides. I assume, because of all my years living in Russia, they think I should be an expert on the subject.

Over the years, the number of men who have contacted me regarding finding a Russian bride is surprising. Most of these men are middle-aged or older, either divorced or never married, and hoping to find a companion to spend the rest of their life with. My heart goes out to these men, because, as a rule, the majority of the Russian mail-order bride business is nothing but a scam run by the Russian mafia.

Once these desperate men show an interest, they are introduced, via email, to five or six Russian women. From the many photographs I have seen, most of these women are absolutely gorgeous—professional models no doubt.

The unsuspecting American will then spend thousands of dollars traveling to and from Russia to meet his prospective bride. The scamming facilitator usually arranges two or three such trips before anything is actually finalized. Of course, most of the money for such expenses goes directly into the pockets of the con artists.

Once the Russian bride has agreed to the marriage, she flies from Russia to America, sometimes with her children from a previous marriage or with a boatload of household goods, all paid for by the prospective groom.

After the marriage takes place, the woman's main interest is in getting a green card. This card allows her to stay, work, and even get welfare benefits while living in the United States. Once the marriage has lasted for a certain period of time, she can apply for citizenship. The U.S. government will then allow her to remain in America indefinitely. That is when the divorce proceedings usually begin.

Against my advice, and surely against the advice of others, several of these men that I have personally met have fallen victim to this awful scheme. Hoping to get married and have someone to share their life with, in the end, the only thing they have to show for their efforts is a depleted bank account and three or four years of heartache and bad memories.

However, to be fair, there are the occasional stories of Russian women who have had sincere intentions but have then suffered abuse at the hands of their American husbands.

THE DARKEST OF SOULS

Surely the saddest situation I hear about is from married couples who stop to visit with me at a Costco signing regarding their heartbreaking experience when trying to adopt a child from Russia. This heartache has been perpetrated on so many unsuspecting would-be parents. Although I understand this adoption scam is happening less and less often, it was never more evident than when Bonnie and I lived in Moscow.

Small in number, we had approximately 100 members in our Moscow Branch made up of Americans, expatriates, and Russians. How we loved our international branch! During those tumultuous years in Russia, not only was it our social and spiritual lifeline, it was also our lifeline to sanity. That wonderful branch allowed us to cope with and survive life in Russia.

With our branch being so small, it was a delight whenever we had "out of town" visitors from America. Often such visitors would be a young couple going through the adoption process in Russia. On their first Sunday in

145

Moscow, when we met them at church, they would be so excited to tell us about their pending adoption. They were always eager to show us photographs they had been exchanging with the child and Russian adoption agency for a year or more. In a few days they anticipated they would meet the child for the first time and, by week's end, they would be flying back home to the States with their newly-adopted child.

Regrettably, many times, we would see that same couple the following Sunday. Their demeanor said it all. Like in so many of these adoption cases, all the initial costs for the adoption had been agreed to and paid for months in advance. However, once the couple arrived in Russia to finalize the adoption and pick up the child, a facilitator within the adoption agency would tell them a mistake had been made, and the couple would not be able to take the child back to the States without paying an additional fee—sometimes as much as $25,000 to $30,000, or more—often double what the adopting parents had already paid.

Understandably, the extortion amount demanded in this game of emotional blackmail is too much for most of the couples to pay. The end result is another dejected Russian child left to survive in an orphanage with little chance of having a family, and a heartbroken couple flying back to the United States with their hopes and dreams dashed. To be kind, these cold, black-hearted villains should all be rounded up, put in a bleak, bare prison cell, and the key thrown into the depths of the Volga River!

SATURDAY NIGHT LIVE

Once in a while, my experiences at book signings are anything but ordinary . . . as in unforgettable!

The only threatening, yet colorful, book signing I've ever done was when Bonnie and I traveled to the Northwest for two weeks.

Headquartered in the state of Washington, Costco has approximately thirty stores there. Their flagship warehouse is next to their corporate offices in Issaquah, fifteen minutes east of Seattle.

On Monday of the second week of signings, Bonnie and I were at one of the Costcos in the downtown area of Seattle. Late in the morning, just before lunch on a somewhat slow day, while sitting at my signing table, I couldn't help but notice two men walking down the aisle towards the book area. I had to force myself not to snicker because both men were dressed like Dan Aykroyd and Steve Martin, right out of a television skit of *Saturday Night Live.*

Sporting their bright, plaid pants, and plaid long-sleeved shirts, they strutted past me like they owned the place. As they walked by, one of them looked my way, stopped, and slowly walked over to my table. Looking down at my book, he asked in a heavy Russian accent,

"What is this?"

In hindsight, that was when I probably made my first mistake.

"Это книга (It is a book)," I replied.

He stared at me with an unforgettable, scathing look, "Do I look like I'm stupid?" he asked.

It was all I could do not to answer in the affirmative.

Whenever I do Costco signings, I use two large posters that depict the cover of my book. The cover shows a man waiting at a desolate Siberian outpost with a train in the background. On the front of the train is the Soviet logo—a hammer and sickle—indicating that it is a Russian or Soviet train. I noticed immediately the man's eyes were transfixed on the logo.

"And what book about?" he asked.

"Sir, the book is about my time living and working in Russia."

"You d___ Americans!" the man exploded, slamming the table with his fist. "You think you know my country. You know nothing of my country!" he exclaimed.

"Well," I said, "with all due respect, I lived in your country for many years. This book is simply about my observations and experiences while I was there."

"And what you do there?" he asked in a loud and contemptuous voice.

"It was my responsibility, to keep track of the KGB and Russian maa........." While almost finishing the sentence, I quickly realized who I might actually be talking to.

"What? I not understand you," he persisted.

Becoming increasingly uncomfortable with the situation, I answered him the same as before, but with more garbled words.

"My job was to keep track of the KGB and blah, blah, blah," I said, covering my mouth while voicing the last few words.

"I CAN NOT HEAR YOU," he yelled. "You in my country doing what?"

The man and his attitude were definitely getting to me. This time, without any babble, I looked directly at him and slowly enunciated each and every word.

"It was my work to keep track of the KGB and Russian mafia."

"Mafia? You write about Russian mafia in book?" he exclaimed loudly.

I looked directly at this Aykroyd/Martin impersonator and answered in the affirmative.

"Yes!"

With his colleague now at his side, the man looked at me with disgust and anger in his eyes, saying,

"Don't you leave; we be right back!"

With that, the two of them stormed out of the Costco.

Yes, I am a believer that miracles still do happen, because in the next thirty minutes, I had signed every last copy of *A Train to Potevka* that particular Costco had in inventory. Bonnie and I quickly gathered up our posters and other items, and within ten minutes we were in our rental car driving across the city of Seattle to the next signing.

When we arrived at the Costco, we told the warehouse manager about the altercation. He was sorry for what had happened but not all that surprised. He told us that in the last several years the Russian mafia had been slowly infiltrating the Seattle area. Their criminal activities had spread to numerous businesses but their real push was in the shipping industry where they were slowly gaining a stronghold. Most of their work involved extortion, insurance fraud, and illegal drugs.

After this Seattle experience, I decided to be a little more careful where I agreed to do my Costco signings; and, also, definitely be more selective with my words when having a conversation with a member of the Russian mafia.

A BOY NAMED TOMMY

A very memorable book signing took place during the weekend of April General Conference a year ago. Because my signings are scheduled months in advance, I inadvertently committed to a signing at the Bountiful Costco on Saturday of conference.

As expected, on Saturday, between the hours of 10:00 AM and 12:00 PM, there were very few people in the warehouse. However, not long after the noon hour, the aisles were packed with shoppers. Because of the many visitors that were in town to attend conference, I was busy signing books almost nonstop.

At around 1:00 PM, a gentleman appeared at my table, dressed in his Sunday best.

"I need to buy one of your books for Tommy," he said. It was obvious he was in a hurry.

"I can do that," I said. "Just tell me how old the boy is you're buying it for, and I'll personalize it accordingly."

Not seeming to pay attention to my remark, the man began to fidget, trying to decide how the book should be signed.

"Okay," he said. "Let's simply make it out to Tommy."

As I prepared to write the name on the endorsement page, he suddenly exclaimed,

"No, no, no . . . that wouldn't be appropriate," he said. Then he began to mumble," How should we do this? What name should we use?"

"Not to worry, sir. Take your time; I'll be happy to sign the book any way you want," I said, trying to put him at ease.

It's only a boy, I thought to myself, *how difficult could it be?*

"The Costco in Salt Lake is sold out of your book. I rushed out here to Bountiful from General Conference," he said. "I've got to get back. We want this book for a family get-together that will take place later this evening. But I just don't know how we should personalize it."

I paused and waited, not wanting to put more pressure on him.

"Should it be 'Tommy' or...?" he struggled with his indecision while repeatedly looking at his watch. Clearly, he was running out of time.

"Okay. Personally, I'd rather it be Tommy, but I think it best that you sign it 'To President Thomas Monson'."

I stood speechless. Recovering my composure, I sat in my chair and personalized the book to President Monson and handed it to the gentleman.

"I'm part of the family through marriage," he explained. "Several of our family have read your book—loved it by the way—and we want to give a copy to Tommy at a family gathering this evening, after conference. Sorry I took up so much of your time . . . but, thank you."

Still at a loss for words, I watched as the man rushed towards the Costco cash registers.

I thought to myself, *What an honor*. Knowing how busy the prophet's life must be and the schedule he has to keep, I wondered if someday President Monson might have the chance to actually read about an American patriot from Bear River, Utah, and his adventures while serving in Russia.

I couldn't help but think back to the late 1980s during my very first assignment into Russia with the Department of State. That weekend I attended my first church meeting in Moscow, there were ten of us there: six Americans and four Russians.

Today, there are tens of thousands of members throughout Eastern Europe, a new temple in Kiev, and seventeen full time missions. As someone who has spent a good portion of his adult life involved with Russia— never could I have dreamed. . . .

.

Chapter 11

BOOK CLUBS AND JELL-O

A good book is the precious lifeblood of a master spirit embalmed and treasured up on purpose to a life beyond life.

John Milton

I will always remember the experience of speaking at my very first book club.

THE FIRST ONE

Potevka had only been out a few weeks when I received a phone call from an elderly lady telling me that everyone in her book club had read *A Train to Potevka*. With those words, she was instantly a friend of mine. She asked if I would be willing to drive to South

154

Salt Lake to spend an hour with her lady friends reviewing and discussing my book.

Her book club had only eight members, but I was extremely flattered just the same. To think they had enjoyed my book enough that they wanted to meet the author and have me answer their questions. Wow!

A few weeks later, I drove to the address of an old home directly south of St. Mark's Hospital where I met these eight beautiful, young ladies. Actually, not one was under eighty-five, but they were an absolute delight. After the hour was over, we ate the staple dessert of Utah; green Jell-O topped with a dab of whipped cream.

This proved to be the first of what seemed to be a thousand book club visits. Within a very short time, the avalanche began. I never dreamed there were so many book clubs in the northern hemisphere, let alone along the Wasatch Front of the Rocky Mountains. For me, it was a way to get the word out about *A Train to Potevka*; for the book clubs, it was a chance to be able to discuss and review their "Book of the Month" personally with the author.

Once the word got out that Mike Ramsdell would speak at book clubs, the phone began to ring off the hook. For the first six months, I was speaking five to six times a week. I remember one particular day speaking to a book club at ten o'clock in the morning in Brigham City, at two o'clock in the afternoon in Logan, and then again, that night, at seven o'clock in Farmington.

Because most of these book clubs averaged only fifteen to twenty people, after the first six months we started suggesting that husbands be invited to participate. What man would not want to hear about the escapades of a Mormon 007? This immediately doubled the number of attendees.

After that first year of speaking primarily to book clubs, organizers began asking me to give my presentation at ward or community activities where both young and old could participate. This eventually led to doing stake events; most of which are very well attended. At one of the more recent gatherings, which included two Arizona stakes, I was honored that there were 1300 people in attendance. Over time, the number of requests have increased to such a degree, it has become impossible to fill them all. It is humbling and encouraging that so many people are interested in hearing a message of patriotism and the blessings of living in America.

After my book first came out, the opportunity to tell my story to book clubs gave me the experience and confidence to speak to larger audiences which, in turn, has led to doing hundreds of presentations around the country. Another benefit from doing these book clubs; some can be downright fun.

AN ENJOYABLE ROOT CANAL?

It's worth sharing the following story which happened with an unsuspecting book club in Davis County. This happened one year ago when I awoke one morning with an aching tooth. I drove to Centerville where my son, Chris, has his dental practice. After checking out the problem tooth, he said,

"Dad, you're going to have to get a root canal."

"Yikes! How long will I have to wait before there's an opening to get that done?" I asked.

"No worries, Dad," he said. "I have a colleague who is an endodontist (a specialist in root canals); he is one of the best. I'm sure we can get you in to see him in the next couple of days."

Thankfully, Chris was able to get me in to see the endodontist that very afternoon. When I walked into Dr. Johnson's office for my appointment, the attractive, middle aged receptionist looked at me like she had just seen a ghost. After a long pause, she stated,

"You're Mike Ramsdell."

"Well, I think I am," I laughed.

"I don't believe this! What a coincidence. My name is Lori, and for the last month I've been living and reliving your journey across Russia. Tonight I'm doing a review on your book for thirty-five women at our book club. They won't believe this!"

Realizing I finally had the chance, perhaps, to pull off something I had thought about so many times before, I asked her,

"Lori, would you consider a crazy idea that I've had floating about in my head for a couple of years now?"

"And what would that be?" she asked.

"Not to take away from the preparation you've done to give a review of my book, but what about this idea? You get started with your presentation and then, without anyone knowing what's about to happen, I'll walk in unannounced. Most won't have any idea who I am."

I could tell she saw in her mind the possibilities by the smile on her face.

"We've got to do it. The ladies won't believe this; they'll be so excited!"

The evening unfolded as if we had been rehearsing it for weeks.

In a beautiful subdivision of Layton, the book club members gathered together at 7:00 PM in the basement of the hostess's beautiful home. At 7:10 PM, Lori began her review of *A Train to Potevka*. At 7:15 PM I walked through the front door. As I descended the staircase and entered the basement, 70 uneasy eyes turned in my direction. With every chair occupied, I sat on the stairs at one end of the room. You can imagine the looks and stares. An uneasy hush came over the room; a man that no one knew had just walked into the basement of a home and sat down among a group of concerned women.

"Please, go on," I said. "Don't worry about me, I'm only here to talk about Amway."

Some of the ladies gave a nervous kind of giggle and looked at one another, still unsure about the stranger in the room.

Lori resumed her review for a few more minutes. As if on cue, one of the women raised her hand and asked,

"Do we know if the agent's wife knew what kind of work he was involved in while they lived together in Russia?"

There were several murmured responses from the members.

"I'm not certain," Lori said, "but why don't we ask Mike himself?"

Suddenly all eyes were looking in my direction.

"Ladies, may I please introduce a new special friend of mine and our surprise guest, Mike Ramsdell."

I stood. They all gave me a warm welcoming applause.

I had planned to stay for only an hour, but after two, I finally said my goodbyes.

What a great evening we had together. They got to meet the author, and I was able to taste another great dessert: green Jell-O.

It was my very first "groupie" experience, and, indeed, they had made me feel like a genuine, bona fide rock star.

What a fun evening!

HIBERNATING IN HEBER

Bonnie and I were excited when we got a phone call from an acquaintance by the name of Viola. We had met her on several occasions when I was doing signings at Costco. She was already a fan of my book and had bought dozens of copies to give to family and friends. She and her husband, Monte, have a beautiful home in Heber Valley. We accepted her invitation to speak to her empty-nesters/book club that would meet together in a couple of weeks.

It was winter at its most beautiful, yet coldest, when we drove into Heber Valley. The entire area was blanketed with a deep snow.

Once all the guests had arrived, we were treated to a huge holiday buffet as only Viola can prepare and, yes, there was green Jell-O. As hosts, Viola and Monte made certain that everyone had their fill, especially, the main invited guests, Mike and Bonnie.

Once the dinner was over and put away, the people assembled in the spacious family room where chairs had been placed throughout to accommodate the large number of guests. While making my way to the front of the crowd, near the huge marbled fireplace, Viola approached me.

"Mike," she said, indicating a spot close to the fire, "this is where I would like you to stand while giving your presentation. And right here next to you," she pointed to a huge, high-back, quilted chair off to the side of the fireplace, "is especially saved for Bonnie."

"Thank you so much," I replied, "but Bonnie usually sits at the back of the room in order to catch up on some paperwork. She's only heard my presentation 300 plus times."

Viola giggled.

The next thing I knew, Viola was escorting Bonnie to the front of the room to her place of honor, the huge, high-back chair. Then Viola disappeared into the crowd to take care of the rest of the guests.

I walked over to Bonnie as she was already snuggling down into her cocoon.

"Bon," I said, "you can't sit there. You'll fall asleep."

"I . . . will . . . not!" she replied, somewhat indignantly.

"Sweetie, you just finished a huge buffet—and I saw how much you ate. In that chair, you're only a few feet from the fireplace; you'll be out in 15 minutes."

"No I won't, don't be ridiculous!" she said. "I'm here to support you, I'll be just fine."

"Bon, trust me. You'll fall asleep. Our lives have been so crazy-busy lately and we've been keeping such late hours traveling to speaking events. Just sit at the back of the room so you can get up and walk around if you need to."

"Nope, I'm staying right here! I'll be fine; quit worrying about it," she replied.

With the guests all settled in their seats, Viola introduced me to the crowd and gave a special introduction of Bonnie, now sitting comfortably in her privileged place—the big, high-back chair.

After Viola's introduction, I began my presentation by thanking them for the invitation to join with them and I made mention of what a special treat it was to have Bonnie with me.

"Usually, when I speak along the Wasatch Front," I told them, "Bonnie stays at home taking care of the responsibilities of the business but mostly to spend time with her three cats: Gorby, Yeltsin, and Putin. When I travel out of state to speak, then Bonnie normally travels with me. So tonight's a special evening that she can join me here."

With everyone ready, I began my presentation about my years in Russia and how the book *A Train to Potevka* came to be.

Not ten minutes into my talk, I glanced over at Bonnie. She had her head laid back, and her body was slouched down in the quilted, comfortable chair; sound asleep. At that moment, I regretted so much that I didn't have my digital camera with me.

Of course, everyone in the room had a perfect view of Sleeping Beauty. I covered for her by telling them,

"You'll have to excuse my Bonnie. We have been so busy these last few weeks with speaking events, movie meetings in California, and putting in some very late hours working on the screenplay."

The audience seemed to understand.

So while Bonnie slept, I shared, with that great group, my story about my time in Russia and how this cold winter's night in Heber Valley reminded me so much of Siberia.

I don't know how close I was to the end of my presentation when she awoke, but I do know this, you could "never" again get her to sit in a big, comfortable, high-back chair next to a roaring fireplace after a delicious holiday buffet on a cold winter's night . . . hibernating in Heber.

She refused to talk to me all the way home.

HERSHEY'S & FINE CHINA

One night at about 11:30 PM, our home phone rang.

At least for me, when someone calls that late at night, it usually means trouble of some sort. Normally, out of respect, due to that late hour, few people in their right mind would make a phone call just to chat.

I picked up the receiver. "Hello?" I said.

A strange female voice which I didn't recognize, was on the other end.

"Hello, may I speak to Mr. Ramsdell?" she asked.

"Speaking," I replied.

"Are you the Mike Ramsdell who wrote *A Train to Potevka*?"

"Yes," I answered, hearing what sounded like a lot of people-noise in the background.

"Mr. Ramsdell, my husband and I just finished your book ten minutes ago. For the last three evenings, we've taken turns reading it together."

"I appreciate your phone call," I said, "but do you realize that it's almost 11:30 at night?"

"I'm sorry that I'm calling so late, but my husband and I have several questions that couldn't wait."

"Ma'am, I really am honored that you and your husband enjoyed my book, but it's still 11:30 at night," I replied, hoping she would get my drift.

"Mr. Ramsdell," she began, "our first question has to do with. . . ."

Who was this crazy lady, and why couldn't she take a hint? Doesn't she have a wrist watch or a clock on the wall? Good grief, most folks are asleep at this hour.

"Ma'am, I'm flattered that you enjoyed the book, but why don't you call me some other time? I'd be happy to answer your questions then," I said, hoping to get rid of her.

"Well, before you hang up, could I ask a favor of you? Is there a chance we could get you to come and speak at our place? We would want to invite a few friends," she said.

With this woman's lack of people skills, I could just imagine the kids and chaos in her home.

"Why don't you call me in the morning, and we'll discuss it," I said, seeing myself, in my mind, standing in her kitchen giving a book review to three weird couples with wild teenagers and little kids running around.

"Thank you, Mr. Ramsdell. It will be an honor to have you here for dinner. I'll call you in the morning."

I hung up the phone, realizing that she didn't even leave her name. And, did I just agree to a dinner engagement?

The following morning, precisely at 8:00 AM, she called back. I reluctantly agreed on a date for the following week.

"I'll email you our address and the directions," she said.

Well, I thought to myself, *at least she owns a computer.*

As always, I turned the final arrangements over to Bonnie.

The following week, with Bonnie using Mapquest as our guide, we stopped in front of the driveway of what had to be one of the largest homes we had ever seen; well over 20,000 square feet. It was then we realized it was the residence of one of the most wealthy families in the entire state. Totally the opposite of what we had expected.

After a tour of her stunning home, our hostess walked us into the dining area where we were amazed to see forty place settings of china and crystal around the table. The room, the decor of dark wood and leather, the paintings on the wall; it was one of the most beautiful dining rooms we had ever seen. In the middle of the table was a beautiful, fresh floral arrangement.

Bonnie and I looked at one another, shaking our heads, and smiled.

There, at each place setting, between the goblet of ice water and the china dinner plate, was a Hershey's with Almonds candy bar.

Yes, indeed, the lady and her husband really had read *A Train to Potevka*.

Chapter 12

KEYNOTES AND FIRESIDES

PROBLEMATIC, POSITIVE, AND PATRIOTIC

And they who for their country die
Shall fill an honored grave,
For glory lights the soldier's tomb,
And beauty weeps the brave.

J. R. Drake

I've had the opportunity to speak at several hundred venues since my book was released. At each event, I try to adapt my remarks to the background of the group to which I'm speaking: who they are, what they represent, their age, their gender, and where the venue takes place.

The following is a compilation of some of the more interesting presentations I have experienced since I wrote *A Train to Potevka*.

PROBLEMATIC

GUESS WHO'S NEXT?

Not long ago, I was asked to address a group of 400 youth in South Salt Lake. As most can well understand, speaking to a group of 14- to 16-year-old teenagers can be very challenging. However, having been through the learning curve of speaking to teens, I now begin with the McDonald's story from my book. This is the story of when I accidentally met two of the first elders sent to Russia to open up Moscow for the preaching of the Gospel and the subsequent events that happened when I took them to eat at the first McDonald's ever built in Russia. All teenagers, of course, seem to relate to McDonald's and, once they hear the story, the youth are usually engaged for the rest of my presentation.

At the beginning of my remarks that particular evening, I told the group of young people,

"If you have questions, please hold them until the end of my presentation. I'll be happy to answer them at that time, during the question-and-answer (Q&A) period."

Halfway through my talk, however, a young man, who was centrally located in the audience, raised his hand. Without acknowledging him, I continued. In total disregard to what I had said, this teenager kept putting his hand up, hoping I would take his question. Needless to say, his behavior was irritating, not only to me but to the rest of those in the audience. When it became clear he was not going to put his hand down, I stopped, and looked in his direction,

"It's obvious you have a question," I said, "but, as I asked at the beginning, I wish you would save it until I finish my presentation. I'll answer it at that time, along with any questions that others might have."

The young man stood up from his seat, and when he did, the entire room became silent.

"But, Mr. Ramsdell," he said, "I just have one quick question before you continue."

"And then, no more interruptions?" I asked.

"I promise, no more interruptions," he said.

By then every eye in the audience was directed at him.

"So what is your question?"

"Brother Ramsdell, could you tell us how many people you killed during your career as a spy?"

I stood at the podium, shocked, but mostly speechless that he would be so tactless as to ask such a question at such a venue.

Where is this delinquent from? I thought to myself, while trying to gather my thoughts. *Bear River?*

Four hundred youth sat totally silent waiting for my response.

Keeping my eyes on him during a long, purposeful pause, I replied,

"Well, let's see . . ." I paused again for effect, looked down at my hand, and started to count out loud on my fingers:

" . . . one—two—three—four . . ."

Then I took a deep breath and tried to give the appearance of adding up figures in my head.

The place got even quieter; you could hear a pin drop. Then I pointed directly at him and said,

"You know . . . actually . . . I've forgotten. But anymore interruptions from you, and you're next!"

It was almost as if the young man and I had choreographed this exchange beforehand, because it got a huge laugh and applause.

The young man was true to his word, and I was able to continue my presentation to its conclusion to that great group of young patriots.

SHOOTING DOWN THE SHARPSHOOTERS

Uncomfortable as it sometimes is, every now and again there will be a sharpshooter in the audience. It is as if his sole purpose in being there is to embarrass me by pointing out errors or misinformation in my presentation.

Recently there was just one such individual in the audience where I was speaking to a large group of adults. During the question-and-answer session, he stood arrogantly with his hands on his hips and stated,

"Mr. Ramsdell, are you trying to have us believe that you speak the Russian language so well that you can go on assignment into Russia and pretend to be a Russian?"

The manner in which he asked the question, I, as well as everyone in the audience, could tell he had an agenda to put me in my place.

As the audience sat quietly, waiting to see how I would respond, I asked him,

"Well, sir, it's quite evident you haven't read my book, have you?"

He began to fidget with his hands and looked down at the floor.

"Because," I continued, "if you had read my book, you would not be asking such a question."

Then I looked out to the audience and asked,

"What was the cover I normally used when I went on assignment into Russia?"

Almost in unison, like a church choir, they answered,

"You went in as a German."

And, of course, their answer was correct.

In most instances, when an agent is operational in another country, he has to have a cover. Because of the years I spent living and working in Germany, I speak fluent German. Therefore, during a number of my assignments into Russia, I went in with a German cover, which I write about in my book, *A Train to Potevka*. My clothes, my documentation, even my luggage, showed me to be German. Whenever the need arose, I would speak Russian to the Russians, but with a heavy German accent.

After the question-and-answer session was over, the male sharpshooter came up to the podium and waited in line to speak to me. When his turn came, he told me he had asked the question, not to embarrass me, but to make a point to the audience. Covering his tracks, he claimed he knew the answer to the question before he asked it. . . . Right.

Dealing with sharpshooters in the audience can, at times, be difficult. At other times, they can add a great deal of fun and color to the presentation.

A *BABUSHKA'S* SCOLDING

Several months ago, while speaking to a large community group, I had an old *babushka* (grandmother) take me to task during the Q&A. When I called on this grandmother to take her question, she asked,

"Mr. Ramsdell, whatever happened to the wife and son of Yuri Novotny?"

As the reader, you might recall that the longest chapter in *A Train to Potevka,* chapter eight, entitled *Bad Karma in Bavaria,* has to do with the years I was assigned as an instructor at the U.S. Intelligence School-Europe in Oberammergau, Germany. It was there that I befriended a student attending our school, a U.S. Air Force captain. As the story unfolds, while making my evening rounds as the staff duty officer on campus, I encountered my friend trying to steal top secret documents from the NATO facility. In a moment of panic after being discovered, he attempted to take his life by cutting both his wrists. It was a tragic event in this otherwise idyllic time, living and working at this top secret school in the German Alps.

My friend Yuri left behind a wife and little boy. Based upon the events that I detail in my book, the grandmother's question was

174

reasonable. However, when I told her that I did not know what had happened to Yuri's wife and little boy, she responded,

"Mr. Ramsdell, while an instructor at the intelligence school, you and Yuri developed a close friendship. How, then, could you possibly be so callous and hardhearted that you didn't care enough to stay in touch with Yuri's wife and little boy after Yuri's death?"

Most having read the book, a hush came over the audience as they waited for my reply.

As the grandma stood in the middle of the audience, looking at me defiantly, I said to her,

"Your question is both logical and appropriate. I can understand how you feel. But I hope you will try to understand and appreciate my position.

As a counterintelligence agent, the U.S. Government had probably spent close to a half million dollars sending me to spy school and, afterwards, to the Russian Institute in Washington, D.C. They also had spent tens of thousands of dollars on other training and qualifying me for a special top secret security clearance.

Inasmuch as I was basically just starting my career, can you imagine what would have happened had my supervisors learned that I maintained contact with the wife of a Russian spy? And remember, as an agent, we were polygraphed on a regular basis."

The old *babushka* sat down.

I continued, "As much as my heart ached for Yuri's wife and son, I had a choice to make. I could terminate any contact I had with Yuri's family and be able to continue my career and have the opportunity, through my service, to give back to the intelligence community that had invested so much in me. Or, on the other hand, I could, as my heart wanted me to do, forget about what had been invested in my career and maintain a relationship with Yuri's wife and son. Needless to say, my career would have been over.

Rarely does a day go by that I do not think about Yuri, his wife, and little boy, and what happened when I was a young lieutenant teaching at the Intelligence School in the German Alps."

It was a special moment when, after the Q&A session, the grandmother came up to me and apologized for her remarks. After a hug, my new friend walked away with her family, hopefully, a little wiser and with a greater appreciation for the world I had worked and lived in for so many years . . . *Russia: Rags and Riches—Spies and Lies.*

DO IT RIGHT

The success of any of these speaking events, corporate or otherwise, depends on the people who are in charge of them. They can work to make it successful and well attended, or they can do very little and, as a result, only a few people will be there to participate.

Approximately a year ago, I received a phone call from a woman asking if I would be willing to speak at a stake event in the Avenues, just northeast of the Capitol Building in Salt Lake City. From our conversation, she seemed very enthusiastic about being in charge and organizing the event. She was certain that over 500 people would be in attendance. I agreed to her request, and then turned the details over to Bonnie, who always asks that events be well advertised.

Attendance for the night of that stake fireside, including those who showed up late, was . . . 20. After my presentation, I was not happy to say the least. I asked the woman in charge what had happened and if the event had been advertised at all.

"Brother Ramsdell," she said, "I just wasn't able to get the word out."

Once again, it all depends on who they put in charge. When such events fall flat, I'm reminded of the old cliché, "If you want to get something done, give it to a busy person."

In contrast to that negative experience, a few months later I was asked to speak in Weber County at a new stake center. The couple in charge of the event was the previous stake president and his wife. Seldom have I seen an event so well organized.

As mentioned, Bonnie handles all my speaking engagements and, once in a while, I've been known to mix up the group I'm speaking to.

On this particular evening, I went to the stake center somehow thinking that I was speaking to a small Relief Society group.

Running a little bit behind schedule, I panicked because there were no parking spaces close by. I had to park along the side of the road, a considerable distance away. When I finally got to the building, I frantically tried to find the outside entrance to the Relief Society room.

"Are you Mike Ramsdell?" a man yelled to me from off in the distance.

"Yes," I replied. "I'm here to speak to the Relief Society. Would you please direct me to the back door?"

"Brother Ramsdell, you're not here to speak to the Relief Society. Please, follow me," he said, as he escorted me into the building and to the front of the chapel.

A professional a cappella group was on the stage, singing patriotic songs. Directly behind them was a row of 16 American flags. As I sat down, I saw a sea of people in front of me. Including the overflow, 600 to 700 people were in attendance. I seldom remember a more patriotic feeling at an event than was there that night. And all the credit goes to the organizational skills and hard work of the former stake president and his wife.

IDAHO SPUDS

After *Potevka* had been out for approximately one year, I received a call from a gentleman in Boise, Idaho.

"Mr. Ramsdell, would you be willing to be the keynote speaker at our fall convention?" he asked.

Wow, I thought to myself. *How cool is this? I'm now being asked to travel out of state to share my experiences and message.*

He continued, "Would $$$$ be enough compensation?"

I sat speechless.

"Besides your keynote compensation, we're planning for you and your wife to stay at the hotel near the convention center and, of course, we will pick up the tab for your room, meals, and all your expenses."

After I was able to get my mouth working again, I told the gentleman,

"Yes . . . of course, I would be honored to speak at your convention. By the way, sir, who are you and what kind of convention is this?" I asked.

"We are the Ranchers/Farmers Association of Idaho."

Immediately my enthusiasm and spirit came crashing down. These people had obviously confused me with someone else.

"Sir," I said, "my book and presentation have nothing to do with ranchers, farmers, or cowboys. I'm very honored, but I'm sure that you have me confused with some other author or keynote speaker."

"But Mr. Ramsdell, didn't you write the book, *A Train to Potevka*?" he asked.

"Yes, I did," I replied.

"Well, a few months ago our director read your book then insisted that everyone on the staff read your book as well. Growing up in the farm country of northern Utah as you did, and ending up working in the spy world in Russia, is a story we all want to hear."

Two months later Bonnie and I traveled to Boise, Idaho, where we spent a wonderful weekend with several hundred Idaho patriots.

One of the highlights of the trip was the Friday night country-western dance. Both Bonnie and I love western music, and she can Texas two-step with the best of them. Me, however . . . I was born with two left feet. Still, we had a great time during our weekend in Boise. And to think, I got paid to be there—my very first paid event.

There is a postscript to this story and Boise, Idaho. It was only a few months later that I was asked to do a fireside at one of the LDS stakes there. The fireside was to take place at a large, new stake center. I was told that because it had been well advertised, they expected 300-plus people to attend.

I arrived at the stake center at 6:30 PM. At 6:50 PM, ten minutes before I was to speak, there were five people in the stake center, and that included me and the stake president, who was getting more nervous by the minute. The prelude music started at 7:00 PM, and people slowly began to arrive and take their seats. By 7:25 the stake center was completely full including the overflow area.

I couldn't help it; my opening remarks had to do with "Mormon standard time."

"I know we have a reputation in Utah for being late to all our church meetings," I told them, "but you Idaho spud farmers have definitely raised the bar!"

POSITIVE

PICKING RASPBERRIES

Whenever I am introduced to an audience, the person giving the introduction usually mentions that I grew up in Bear River, Utah. Often, after my presentation, people will come up to me and say,

"Mike, I know exactly where you grew up. Each year during the summer our family goes up there to pick raspberries."

Then I have to tell the person they were not quite correct. They were 70 miles off. Bear River, where I grew up, is not Bear Lake, famous for its raspberry milkshakes.

For those who do not know where Bear River is, it's a small farming and ranching community with a few hundred families, located halfway between Tremonton and Brigham City in northern Utah. To me, Bear River will always be home, where some of the best people in the world live. I wouldn't trade the years I grew up there for anything.

A BEAR RIVER COWBOY

When I was a boy my family lived on the north end of town in Bear River; my best friend was Rawlin Andersen. Being the same age and living only a quarter of a mile apart, we were like Siamese twins, inseparable. His dad was a rancher, and as such, Rawlin, of course, had a horse. The name of the horse was Floss.

In the summers when we were out of school for the three-month break, we were like Huckleberry Finn and Tom Sawyer. Riding together bareback, the two of us lived on that horse. We spent our summer days racing Floss up and down the back roads of our little town, saving the wagon train from Black Bart and his bandits, floating our log rafts along down the Bear River, skinny dipping at the swimming hole, and trying our best to find whatever mischief we could. We were absolutely best childhood friends.

When I was about nine or ten years old, my family moved to the middle of town where my dad had opened a small, truck stop cafe—Pop's Place. Rawlin and I, although in the same grade at school, slowly drifted apart, especially during our high school years. I became heavily involved in school sports and student council; he was heavily involved in horses and being a rodeo cowboy.

Spending his career at Thiokol (a company that built rocket boosters for NASA), along with a six-year stint with the National Guard, he has remained a genuine cowboy his entire adult life: always involved with rodeos, horses, cattle, and sheep. In his younger years, besides competing in local-area rodeos, he was a member of the Box Elder County Sheriff's Posse. Living a hard, tough, cowboy life, he has been banged up, kicked around, and suffered his share of broken bones. And, like all of us, his body has worn with age. He now even limps like a real cowboy. I hadn't seen my childhood friend for years.

A few years ago, I had the opportunity to return to my hometown of Bear River to give a presentation about my career and book at the local church. For me, it was a wonderful evening with probably 200 to 300 people in attendance.

Because I grew up there and knew so many of those who were in the audience, I was heartened to see, when I concluded my talk, probably forty to fifty people forming a line near the podium to say "hi" and shake my hand.

The line moved ever so slowly; there was so much to say, but so little time. Plus, I was eager to start my long drive back to Davis County and get home to Bonnie.

As I looked down the column of people, I couldn't believe it; there was my childhood friend, Rawlin Anderson. Dressed in a classic western jacket, Levi's, and cowboy boots; he was the last person waiting in line.

Finally, after twenty minutes or so, with almost everyone gone, he stepped towards me. We stood for a moment, not saying a word. We just smiled and looked at one another, shaking our heads, of course, thinking: *How long has it been?*

He opened his coat jacket and stuck his thumbs down in his belt—like cowboys do. In the middle of that belt was the biggest, most beautiful, silver cowboy belt buckle I had ever seen.

He stepped closer.

"So . . . you're a writer," he said in a slow, cowboy drawl.

I looked at him, waited awhile, and stepped in even closer.

"Yup, I'm a writer," I said, mimicking his words, "but not a 'rider' like I used to be; hanging on for dear life while you galloped old Floss up and down the dirt and gravel roads of Bear River, chasing bandits and bad guys with our cap guns."

He then let go of his belt, reached out and put one arm on my shoulder, and whispered,

"Hell, I grew up with you. I didn't know you could read, let alone write!"

We spent the next half hour sitting in the chapel, discussing the different paths we had taken in life, our families, careers, Russia, and rodeos.

What a great way to end the evening . . . reminiscing with my childhood best friend!

MORRIS, MIKE, AND MACBETH

As I acknowledged earlier, during my high school years, I really did not apply myself academically like I should have, which I still regret to this day. My priorities were hanging out with my best friends, football, student council, dating, and other sports.

When I think back on my senior year and the needless trouble I caused my high school English teacher, Mr. Morris, it makes me feel bad. I got along with all my teachers except for him. For whatever reason, he and I never saw eye-to-eye; and English was my least favorite subject. I saw no use for it. Besides, who cared if I knew about dangling participles, metaphors, Longfellow, and Steinbeck? Why should I bother with *Macbeth;* I was going to be a high school football coach.

A few years ago, I was one of the keynote speakers at the Northern Utah Republican

Convention, held in the new auditorium of my old high school. As the local state chairman introduced me, he told the audience about the national literary success of a Bear River High graduate.

When I stood at the podium, I stated,

"Ladies and Gentlemen, this is the first time I have been back inside the high school since graduating from Bear River. After that introduction, how I wish that Mr. Morris, my high school English teacher, was still alive. He would have been proud . . . but mostly shocked."

As I said these words, I noticed that a quiet buzz went throughout the audience. When I finished my remarks, a dozen or more people came up to me,

"Mike, Mr. Morris is still alive. He's not in an assisted living facility, as you might expect; he still lives by himself in his family home in Tremonton."

Then and there I decided I would pay him a visit and present him with a personalized copy of *A Train to Potevka*. I wanted to thank him for his efforts to introduce me to great literature and the world of writing. Of course, in my case, this was a *real* stretch; but it didn't matter, I was sure he would not remember me anyway.

Certain he would have no clue who I was, I asked Ward Taylor, one of my best friends from high school, to go with me when I visited Mr. Morris. Ward owned the local mortuary in town, had served as stake president, and was very active in the community. I was sure Mr. Morris would certainly recognize Ward when we paid him a visit.

Approximately one month later, just before the Christmas holidays, I traveled back home to Bear River for a missionary farewell. When I called Ward after the Sunday church service to arrange to pick him up for our visit to Mr. Morris, Ward informed me that he had another obligation that prevented him from going with me.

There is no way I can go alone, I convinced myself. *Mr. Morris won't remember me at all, and it will be too awkward otherwise.*

I left Tremonton and had driven halfway to Brigham City when I decided to go back. It really didn't matter if Mr. Morris remembered me or not; I wanted him to have the copy of my book which I had already personalized for him.

Twenty minutes later I was sitting in my car, in front of his house, reviewing in my mind how the conversation might go:

I would hold the book up, cover towards him, and say,

"Mr. Morris, I'm sorry to bother you. My name is Mike Ramsdell. A long time ago I was a student of yours at Bear River High School.

A few years ago, I wrote my first book, which, has become a best seller. I wanted to stop by to thank you for your efforts by giving you this personalized copy of my book."

Though somewhat uneasy, after a few rehearsals, I thought I had my introduction ready.

I walked to his front door, knocked, and waited. Nothing. More knocking. More nothing. After a few minutes, just as I was ready to turn and leave, I heard slow, shuffling footsteps moving toward the door. A moment later the door opened. There stood the man I had caused so much grief as a high school teenager so many years ago.

"Good evening, Mr. Morris," I began. "My name is Mike Ramsdell and . . ."

He looked at me, then looked down at the book.

"I've read it and I loved it," he said, as he swung open the door. "Please, please come in."

For the next half hour we sat in his living room and talked about his years of teaching, literature, the joys of a good book, his favorite authors, and, of course, *A Train to Potevka*. As he walked me to the door, he told me how proud he was of my accomplishment.

"But, for your next book," he said, "you've got to be more disciplined and do a better job with the editing." We had a good laugh over that.

As I shook his hand to bid him farewell, he turned his head away to hide his emotions. I think it meant a lot to him for me to have paid him a visit after all. Knowing I would probably never see this fine man again, I repeated my words of appreciation and gratitude, then told him goodbye.

As I made the hour drive back to my home that night, I reflected on how glad I was that I had gone back to see him. Perhaps my visit made up in some small way for the problems this teenage kid from Bear River had caused him so many years ago.

THE KINGSTON TRIO

Not long ago, I had the opportunity to speak at a teachers conference at the University of Utah. After my introduction as the keynote speaker, I shared with them the following story with the goal in mind to honor them and their profession.

I grew up as the youngest child in a struggling family, in the little town of Bear River, in northern Utah. I was totally lost in our large family, and I'm not exaggerating when I say "lost."

190

Some weekends, for example, when I would get home from grade school, I remember packing a few peanut butter and jelly sandwiches in a sack, grabbing my sleeping bag, sneaking the 22 rifle (I was six/seven years old) from the gun rack in the attic bedroom, and stealing some 22 shells from my older brothers' sock drawers. Then, with my dog, Smooch, for company, I would head down to the Bear River approximately a mile or so away. Sometimes I would meet my best friend Rawlin there, sometimes not. If it was good weather, I would stay out for at least one night, on occasion, two nights. Whenever I returned home, seldom would anyone in my family know I had been gone. As I said, I was totally lost in my family.

Inasmuch as my older brothers were, on average, twelve years older than I, they would often tease me,

"You weren't even born in this family. Mom and Dad picked you up from the side of the road while we were traveling through an Indian reservation."

Of course, whenever I got out of line, they would threaten me,

"You'd better shape up, boy, or Dad's going to take you back to the reservation and leave you."

Growing up feeling basically invisible, I'm certain, had something to do with my life-long struggle with low self-esteem and low self-worth. However, as I explained in chapter four, when I got to high school, I met a teacher who was a great role model for me and helped to change my life: my football coach, Gerald Simmons.

Coach made such an impression upon me at that young age, I determined that for my life's career, I wanted to do one of two things (remember, I'm addressing this large audience of educators): I wanted to be either a teacher—high school football coach—or the banjo player for the Kingston Trio. This, naturally, got a big laugh from the audience, most of whom were around my age.

Why the banjo player for the Kingston Trio? During my teenage years, folk music was the rage throughout the country; and the Kingston Trio was the group that brought it to the forefront of American popular music.

In my book, *A Train to Potevka,* I write about how, as a young boy, I discovered an old guitar in my grandpa's attic. After repairing it, putting on new strings, and tuning the guitar, learning how to play it came quite easily. I have wonderful memories of my years in high school and college when I sang in a number of different folk groups.

Addressing that group of five hundred educators, I told them,

"I never did become a high school teacher or football coach, and I never did become the banjo player for the Kingston Trio. Life took me in another direction. However, this very morning, I received the following email."

Dear Mike,

While on a recent trip to Utah, a friend of mine purchased several copies of your book, "A Train to Potevka." He had you personalize one of the books for me. I was mesmerized by your story and found it inspiring. Mike, your book makes me want to be a better person.

Your references in the book to the Kingston Trio brought a smile to my face. At times when I am questioning my own personal and spiritual direction, I find that the music from the folk era gives me comfort and inspires me to new directions.

Mike, I hope to meet you some day, and, if you are so inclined, please check our concert tour schedule on our website. Whenever we are performing in a city across this great country where you are doing a book signing, I would love to have you and your wife as my personal guests.

Signed, George Grove

Banjo Player of the Kingston Trio

At the podium, I held the email high above my head, declaring:

"Ladies and Gentlemen, I have finally arrived!"

There was laughter, applause, and even a few whistles in response.

Now, the rest of the story.

I was so honored by his email, that, a few days later I sent George Grove a reply and thanked him and told him how honored I was that he enjoyed my book.

He emailed me back.

Mike,

If you are ever here in Las Vegas, where my wife and I live, we would love to invite you and your wife to our home for dinner. And, from time to time, our Trio performs here in Las Vegas. So, if you are ever down here, please check our concert schedule. I truly would like to have you and your wife as my personal guests at our concert.

He included his cell phone number in his email.

Three or four months later, I was doing Costco book signings in southern Utah, Nevada, and Arizona. While signing in St. George, Bonnie reminded me of George Grove's letter and the fact that, during the following four days, I would be signing at the Costcos in Las Vegas.

"Why not call George Grove?" Bonnie said. "Maybe he's home and not on tour right now."

"No way," I said. "Surely he's busy."

Bonnie got out her Blackberry, looked up the Kingston Trio on the Internet, and checked their concert schedule. What a coincidence! For the first time in three years, the Trio was performing at one of the big Las Vegas casino showrooms.

With Bonnie's prompting, I reluctantly called his cell phone number. He was not there so I left a message. Moments later, my cell phone rang. I looked down at the screen; it was George Grove.

"Mike," he said, "I've got some bad news and some good news. The bad news is that our concert is completely sold out; the good news is that you and Bonnie have seats right up front."

A couple of nights later, Bonnie and I were at a sold out concert hall center in Las Vegas, Nevada, listening to the Kingston Trio perform. Although they have been singing together for decades, their voices and harmony have truly improved with age, and they sounded better than ever.

Near the end of the concert, George Grove stepped to the microphone and personally introduced Bonnie and me to the packed audience. He even gave me a plug about my book and that a movie was in the works.

He then dedicated a song to us which, to this day, is still my favorite of all the Kingston Trio songs: "Chilly Winds." Bonnie has promised that this song will be performed when I finally lay my bones down in the cold Bear River ground.

After the performance was over, Bonnie and I were invited to a private party at the casino. We spent the evening swapping stories, sharing favorites folksongs, and meeting the wives and family of the Trio members.

After such a memorable evening, sleep did not come easily. I thought back on my lifelong love of folk music, and the several groups I had sung with. A teenage dream of mine had finally come true. This very night I had been on stage with The Kingston Trio.

Life is good. And, at times . . . really good!

JOHN STEINBECK

The most meaningful honor I have received since writing my book—no, Oprah has not called—was to be one of the guest speakers at the annual *Author's Table* symposium of the John Steinbeck Foundation in Monterey, California. You might ask, how in the world was Mike Ramsdell, a first-time author, invited to speak at the John Steinbeck Foundation?

Well, here is how it happened.

The husband of a woman who sat on the foundation's board of directors was flying from San Francisco to New York. When he boarded the plane and got to his seat, there was my book, *A Train to Potevka,* which someone had left behind. Having forgotten to bring reading material for his long, six-hour flight across the country, he decided to give *Potevka* a try. Just prior to landing at JFK, he finished the book.

Knowing that his wife and the Steinbeck Board of Directors were about to select authors who would be invited to speak at their fall convention, he told his wife about the book *Potevka* and suggested that all the board members should read it before making a final decision about the symposium speakers. The next week I got the phone call inviting me and Bonnie to Monterey.

197

A few months later, I stood at the convention center podium telling about my journey as a young boy filled with dreams from a small town in the Rocky Mountains to that moment of addressing the audience at the Steinbeck Foundation. What an honor!

Earlier, while waiting to be introduced and looking out over all the people, I couldn't help but think how proud my mom would have been to be there with me. I also thought about my brothers and the other naysayers who were so critical of me thinking that I could write a book. Their words still ring in my ears today, especially . . .

"Who do you think you are that anyone is going to care what you have to say?"

That night in Monterey, California, looking out over that large gathering of people, I couldn't help but answer . . .

"Well, it looks like there are a few folks who *do* care what I have to say after all."

The ocean, the beauty of the surrounding area, meeting and mingling with members of the Steinbeck Foundation, visiting with other best-selling authors, and autographing copies of my book . . . it was the perfect evening.

Even better than this, the Foundation invited me back the next year to be the keynote speaker for their annual fundraiser gala.

The John Steinbeck Foundation . . . now that's good company to be in. Even Mr. Morris would agree.

PATRIOTIC

A POTEVKA THANKSGIVING

One of the most memorable speaking events I ever attended was in Provo, Utah.

A few months before Thanksgiving, I was personally contacted by a stake president asking to schedule a fireside. He had already read *Potevka* and was a big fan. At his request, we agreed that I would speak to his stake the week before Thanksgiving.

In the weeks leading up to the fireside, those coordinating the event sent out fliers to all the wards in the stake. I was grateful when I found that, in the flyer, the stake president had praised my book and recommended that those interested should read it before attending.

When I arrived in Provo the evening of the event, I learned that the fireside would not be taking place in the chapel but in the cultural hall, which had been beautifully decorated for Thanksgiving. Over 80 large tables were located throughout the hall with 8 chairs at each table. Each table had place settings which included a plastic fork, knife, spoon, a small paper cup, and a napkin.

When the stake president got up to speak, he asked how many in the congregation had read my book. It appeared that over half of those present had read or were reading *Potevka*.

When the stake president introduced me, he asked me to confine my remarks to the Thanksgiving I had experienced in the village of Potevka, Russia, several years earlier.

When I concluded, the stake president then addressed the audience about the blessings of living in America, the land of plenty, and how grateful we all should be. His most penetrating comment; each night over half the population of the world goes to bed hungry.

As if that statement was some sort of signal, the doors adjoining the kitchen area suddenly opened and 20 teenage girls, dressed in white smocks, carried large round trays of food into the cultural hall. At each table setting, they placed a small paper plate. On the plate was a single spoonful of macaroni and cheese, one small artichoke heart, a sacrament cup containing a few frosted flakes, and a small piece of chocolate broken from a Hershey's with Almonds candy bar. (Those who have read *A Train to Potevka* will relate.)

It was as if all those gathered in the cultural hall didn't know how to react. Some laughed, others moaned, but most remained silent as they ate their humble, *Potevka* Thanksgiving meal.

When it was evident that most people had finished their meager holiday treat, the stake president, again, addressed the congregation. He reminded us all of how blessed we are to live in America and to have such abundance, and that we should always remember those throughout the world who are less fortunate.

With those remarks, most of us thought the evening was over, including myself. However, as the final act for the evening, once again the doors of the cultural hall opened and the girls reappeared, accompanied by 20 adult women, each carrying huge serving trays of food.

Within minutes, large holiday paper plates and cups replaced the small ones at each table, along with all the customary cuisine for a proper Thanksgiving feast: roast turkey with dressing, baked ham, yams, potatoes and gravy, buttered corn, and hot rolls. To top off the evening's banquet was the traditional holiday pumpkin pie, of course, with whipped cream for topping. Not one spoonful of green Jell-O in sight!

What a marvelous evening it was. I couldn't imagine all the planning, work, and effort that went into putting together such an unforgettable event.

Whenever the Thanksgiving holiday rolls around, of course, my thoughts return to my experience years ago in the village of Potevka.. However, I will always remember the kindness of that Provo stake presidency and the evening I spent with those wonderful people celebrating the bounty and blessings of Thanksgiving in America.

RED, WHITE, AND BLUE SNOWFLAKES

The largest group I have ever spoken to was in Snowflake, Arizona, where I was recently asked to be the keynote speaker at a community event commemorating 9/11. As some might remember, Bonnie and I were in New York the morning of the terrorist attacks on the Twin Towers.

As the town of Snowflake is relatively small, all of the other surrounding communities were invited to participate. The committee putting on the event had advertised for months. They were hoping for at least 300 people for the commemoration. Amazingly, that evening there were 1300 people in the audience; approximately 1000 in the community stake center and another 300 at a nearby church where the presentation was broadcast using a live television feed. A testament that patriotism and love of country are still alive and well in America.

It was a special evening for all of us to honor those who died on 9/11 and those who are tasked with the responsibility to safeguard our nation today, especially our military young men and women. I firmly believe those in the military who serve our country, past or present, are our true heroes. We can never thank them and their families enough for the sacrifices they make each day to preserve our great nation.

At the close of all my presentations, I ask for a commitment from each person in the audience.

"The next time you find yourself at an airport, a Costco, or a 7-Eleven, and you see a young man or woman in a military uniform walking towards you, I ask you, please—and this can be a bit clumsy and awkward—please put yourself in front of them, reach out, shake their hand, and tell them how thankful you are for their service. I can tell you from my own experience, you will never know how much such a handshake and a sincere 'Thank you' will mean to those heroes."

PICKING UP THE TAB

Continuing with the same patriotic theme as in the previous story, I have related the following anecdote at several of my presentations:

Not long ago, I was a speaker at a world language conference. The person who gave the keynote address, Dr. Elwin Ingley, was from the East Coast. Flying halfway across the country to our conference, he had a four-hour layover at Chicago's O'Hare Airport.

While at O'Hare, he decided to grab some lunch at one of the airport restaurants. As he was being escorted to his table, he noticed a small group of men and women in military uniform having lunch a few tables away. When the waiter came to take his order, Dr. Ingley pointed to the table where the military group sat.

"I need you to do me a favor, please," he said. "When that table has finished their lunch, I want you to bring me their bill."

The waiter paused. "I'm unable to do that, Sir," he replied.

"What do you mean you're unable to do that? Obviously the men and women seated at that table are serving in our military. I want to pay for their meals," he quickly responded.

"I'm sorry, sir. I can't do that . . . "

Interrupting, Dr. Ingley pulled an American Express card from his wallet and handed it to the waiter.

"I don't understand this," he said. "Take my card. Go ahead, verify that it's valid and that I have funds in my account," he said.

The waiter looked at him, paused again, then said,

"Sir, I can't do that. I'm sorry, but the reason I can't do that is the fact that there are four people ahead of you wanting to pay for their lunch."

I love that story. And I've heard other stories just as uplifting.

There's an account of military men and women returning to Salt Lake International from the Middle East War on a commercial aircraft. As they departed the plane and entered the terminal, a respectful silence became evident throughout the boarding area, muffling the hustle and bustle of everyday life. Hundreds of passengers created a pathway for the exiting soldiers to walk through as the crowd applauded in appreciation.

The above two stories show what America is all about. May God bless each and every person serving, or who has served, in the military. And may God continue to bless our great country, the United States of America.

AGGIE PATRIOTS

When I think of patriotism, a special experience comes to mind that I had when I was asked to speak at my alma mater, Utah State University. The professor who was my sponsor for the event called one evening and asked if I would be willing to address the student body at USU.

"Of course," I told him. "As an alumnus, I would be honored to be back on campus and share some of my experiences with the students."

Near the end of our telephone conversation, he added a warning,

"Just to let you know, there will likely be hecklers in the audience: the anti-war, anti-government, anti-America types."

"Well, my presentation is very patriotic and very pro-America. A few hecklers won't bother me, but thanks for the warning," I responded.

That evening while lying in bed I thought,

Hecklers at Utah State? What's the world coming to?

One month later I was on campus at USU. It had been years since I had been there. The auditorium was completely full by the time my sponsor introduced me. Remembering the professor's words one month earlier regarding the possible hecklers that could be in the audience, I decided to resolve the problem before I even got started.

"I'm honored to be with you today and to be back on the campus where I spent four busy, exciting, wonderful years getting my undergraduate degree. Since leaving Utah State many years ago, my life and career have taken many twists and turns. Growing up in a very patriotic family, I always wanted to serve in the military. I ended up serving for more than 20 years in the Intelligence Corps plus several additional years with other government agencies. I had the opportunity to specialize in Russia, the former Soviet Union, as a counterintelligence agent. I stand before you as a patriot. Despite the multitude of problems we are facing today in America, I want you to know that I love my country. I'm proud to be an American. And so I ask, if you are going to have a problem with my remarks and intend to disrupt my presentation, please leave the auditorium now."

As I scanned the audience, not one person got up to leave.

"Thank you," I said. "Now I'd like to share with you some of the experiences of my career." I began my presentation.

When I concluded my remarks, at least 40 to 50 students formed a line near the podium to shake my hand. Knowing that some of them would probably be late for their next class, I was touched by their warm response to my comments about the blessings and opportunities we have living here in America.

After I had shaken the hands of approximately half of those waiting in line, I extended my hand to the next student, a beautiful young woman in her early twenties. Unlike the other students, she did not offer her hand, which caught me off guard.

"Mr. Ramsdell," she said, "I would rather not shake your hand."

Somewhat startled, I paused.

"You know . . . that's OK," I said. "That's what makes America great. You can have your beliefs and opinions, and I can have mine."

"But . . . you don't understand," she said. "The reason I don't want to shake your hand is because I'd like to give you a big hug instead."

After an embrace, she stepped back and made a statement that still resonates in my ears today.

"Mr. Ramsdell, we young people do not appreciate America. We don't hear enough good about America either. The majority of the time, when watching the news or reading the national headlines, we only hear about the problems in our country and why America is to blame for all the ills and calamities in the world."

Driving home that afternoon from Logan, I couldn't help but think about what this young woman had said. Regrettably, she was right.

It bothers me that the lives of our young people are so busy, with their time taken up by friends, school, studies, sports, TV, movies, computers, video games, iPods and iPads, etc., etc. When do our young people ever have the time to think about or appreciate how fortunate they are to live in this great country?

I strongly feel that we as parents and grandparents need to seize the chance, whenever it presents itself, to help our young people understand the sacrifices that so many have made to preserve our liberties and freedoms, even with their own blood.

Freedom is not free. Our young people need to appreciate just how fortunate they are to live in America; they need to understand what it means to be a patriot.

Chapter 13

CLANDESTINE Q&A

My candle burns at both ends;
It will not last the night;
But, ah, my foes, and, oh, my friends—
It gives a lovely light.
                    Edna St. Vincent Millay

Whenever I'm asked to speak, I usually coordinate with the sponsor of the event to have a question-and-answer (Q&A) session at the end. This normally lasts from 15 to 30 minutes. It is my favorite part of the presentation, and there have been times when the Q&A period has lasted for more than an hour.

Many times, it has been suggested during the Q&A that I put down on paper the answers to the most frequently asked questions. Thus, when I determined to write this book of short stories, I decided to include a chapter regarding such Q&A information.

I hope you will find this chapter interesting, enjoyable, and worth reading.

ONLY THE SHADOW KNOWS

COVERT COVER

- What did your family think you were doing all those years in Russia?

Working in the covert world as an agent, one always has to have a cover. My family understood that I was the Director of the American Trade Center in Moscow, Russia, and the manager of the Radisson Hotel, which was part of the Trade Center complex.

During the fall of the Soviet Empire, millions of government workers were not paid their salaries for six months or longer because of the collapse of the Soviet economy and the devaluation of the Russian ruble. The unpaid and jobless included thousands of KGB employees.

Desperate to find employment, many of these former KGB, who spoke fluent English and many other foreign languages, were hired on at the Trade Center. Within months, this multinational complex was swarming with former KGB agents. The reason? These workers, who were paid an average of $30.00 a month under the Soviet system, were now being paid, as employees of the Trade Center, ten times their old KGB salary.

While U.S. Intelligence monitored the breakup of the old Soviet Union and the myriad changes that were taking place in Russia, the U.S. Department of State determined that they needed to have extra pair of eyes and ears on the inside to monitor the activities of the KGB.

During this very same time period, an advertisement appeared in the *Moscow Times* looking for applicants to interview for the position of Assistant to the Director of the Trade Center. Through our connections with the U.S. Embassy in Moscow, I was hired on to fill that position. It would be a job with little actual responsibilities. My main focus would be to monitor the activities of the former KGB agents and the companies they now worked for.

Two days after I reported for work at the Trade Center and was introduced as the assistant to the director, the director himself suffered a serious stroke and was medivacked back to the United States. The next day I was called in to a meeting of the Board of Directors, half of whom were Russian and the other half American, and summarily assigned the job as the new director of the American Trade Center.

This, of course, presented a huge problem. I now had the responsibility of overseeing the entire operation of the Trade Center, which included a personal staff of 6 Russians, 16 expatriate department heads, 16 deputies who were all Russians, and a workforce of 1400 Russian employees. Adding to the complexity of the situation, I still had the assignment to monitor the activities of the hundred or so former KGB agents now working at the Trade Center. Needless to say, I had my hands full.

Several mornings each week, my staff thought I was working out, playing racquetball at the U.S. Embassy. Several evenings each week, they thought I was having dinner with Bonnie at the embassy cafeteria. For a period of three years, I wore these two hats, juggling all the responsibilities that came with both sides of this unusual situation.

Therefore, when asked by family or friends as to what I was doing during my years in Russia, I could honestly answer: (1) I was working as the director of the American Trade Center, or (2) managing the Radisson Hotel in Moscow.

LIVING WITH A SPOOK

- Did Bonnie know you were working as a covert agent while in Russia?

Bonnie and I first met when she was hired on as the receptionist/office manager for our small international consulting firm in Salt Lake City. During the years she worked for us, she had no idea that other work was being conducted besides consulting. Because of our working relationship, Bonnie knew I had to travel from time to time, both domestically and abroad, but she never imposed herself or questioned me about the reason for my frequent trips. I'm certain she had an idea I was involved in some kind of security work, but she never asked specifics as to what I was doing. I always appreciated her attitude in this regard, as there were things which were off-limits, things I could not talk about.

Years later, while I was serving in Russia, Bonnie came to Europe to spend Christmas with me in the German Alps. It was there in Bavaria where our love story really began. Bonnie and I were married by a Finnish constable in the old courthouse near downtown Helsinki. After our wedding ceremony, held 7000 miles from home, the two of us celebrated our marriage with a dinner at a famous Finnish Chinese restaurant. What a wonderful evening! Our only regret was that our family and friends were not there to celebrate with us.

After the our dinner, I felt it an appropriate time to address my career work with Bonnie. I remember the conversation like it was yesterday.

"Bon, as we start this journey together, if you have any questions about my work, now's the time to ask. I'll try to answer as best I can, but, as you know, there are some things which I cannot discuss."

"Mike," she said, reaching across the table and putting her hand on mine, "you don't have to tell me a thing. I do request, however, if there's that 'one chance' you might not come back from an assignment, please tell me before you go. That way, I'll know what happened if you don't make it back."

This reaction was so typical of Bonnie. I had her full support back then, and it has remained so throughout our marriage. She is one of the most remarkable people I have ever known, and I am so proud to be her husband.

It was during this time that she really showed her true mettle. After our marriage, where did we go on our honeymoon . . . Rome? Hawaii? Paris? *Nyet*. . . . We went into Russia and stayed for six years.

Bonnie is the oldest in a family of 12 brothers and sisters. I can only imagine how she missed her parents and siblings. Yet, never once in all those years of living in Russia did she ever complain. I knew then, definitely, that this was the woman I wanted to spend the rest of my life with.

ONLY IN VEGAS!

• Are you and Bonnie still married?

Strange as it may sound, I am often asked this question. Yet, I have to admit the question most often comes up when I'm doing signings or speaking at an event in Las Vegas, Nevada. In my opinion, it must come with the territory. When I'm doing book signings in other states and asked that question, I, in turn, ask: "Where are you from . . . Las Vegas?"

It bothers me to think that, for whatever reason, a reader of *Potevka* somehow decided that a long-term marriage between Bonnie and me was not possible. Giving the benefit of the doubt to those who pose such a question, I remind myself of the difficult culture that exists for those who work in the covert world. Disheartening, yet true, the men and women working in intelligence have one of the highest, if not the highest, suicide and divorce rates of any other profession. So, perhaps, being asked, "Are you and Bonnie still married?" is not all that inappropriate.

Final answer . . . yes, my dear Bon and I are still married and still enjoying every day of this incredible "train" journey we are traveling together.

THE MOVIE

SACRAMENTO

● How did the movie come about?

A few years ago Bonnie and I were asked to travel to Sacramento, California, where I had the opportunity speak to an assemblage of six adjoining stakes. It was just after my presentation that I noticed a man almost rushing unexpectedly towards the podium where I was standing. Pointing while looking up at me he said:

"I have no idea who you are. I have never read your book. In fact, I have never even heard of your book. But based on your presentation this evening, your story needs to be made into a movie."

Looking down from the podium at the man, I pointed at him and said,

"Well I don't know who you are. And I don't know if you've written a book. But based on what you just said . . . I've always really liked you . . . a lot!"

The man standing below me was none other than Academy Award-winning director Kieth Merrill. It was from that initial meeting that the seeds of turning *A Train to Potevka* into a movie began to grow. Within weeks Kieth Merrill had made contact with his colleagues, the Rancie Brothers, in Melbourne, Australia, who in turn read the book and flew to America to negotiate the rights to take *Potevka* to the movie screen.

Interestingly, for the two to three months that we negotiated the terms of the contract for the film, Bonnie and I were very impressed with our new Australian friends. During this entire time neither their religion nor their church affiliation was never discussed. It was several weeks after signing the contract when, much to our surprise, we learned that these new friends from Down Under were members of the LDS faith. Now, we had a lot more in common than just a movie.

One of the highlights that happened during one of our pre-production meetings was when Bonnie and I were told that we would have the opportunity to do a cameo in the film. However, we would be on screen for only 30 to

60 seconds. Totally unexpected, you can imagine how excited we were when told this news. Also, we were informed that we could choose the scene, within reason of course, in which we would appear.

For weeks and weeks, after getting this news, we racked our brains trying to come up with the appropriate scene for our cameo. Then, while driving home late one night from a speaking engagement in Springville, it came to me.

I got so excited, I put the pedal to the metal, wanting to get home as soon as possible to tell Bon about my idea. When I had worked out the details of the cameo in my mind, I called her on my cell phone.

"Hello, Sweetie," she said.

"You'd better wait up for me and not go to bed," I told her. "I've got some great news you'll love to hear."

"Well, what is it . . . can't you tell me now?" she asked.

"Nope, you've got to wait," I replied. "I'll tell you when I get home; but it has to do with our movie."

When I pulled in the garage she was waiting at the top of the landing near the kitchen. Once inside, I explained my idea for our on-camera appearance. She was so excited she got out of her PJs and took me to McDonald's for a late-night, milkshake celebration.

When you see the movie, *A Train to Potevka*, there will be a scene right out of the book where Bonnie and I are invited to the New Year's Eve Ball at the American Embassy in Helsinki. On the screen you will see the ballroom, the orchestra, diplomats, honored guests, and the embassy Marine Guard personnel dancing, celebrating, and welcoming in the New Year. If you watch closely, for a brief moment, you will see the real Mike Ramsdell dressed in his officers dress blues and beautiful Bonnie in her holiday formal waltzing—provided they can teach me how—across the ballroom dance floor. Yes, we are excited!

And, yes . . . I have been practicing.

PITT OR PEE-WEE

• Who is going to play Mike in the movie?

You can, perhaps, imagine how exciting it was for Bonnie and me when we were first approached by a movie company which wanted to turn my book, *Potevka,* into a major motion picture.

It was probably only a year after the book came out that we were contacted by several film studios about buying the movie rights. After months of discussions with several potential movie companies, we finally signed with Audience Alliance Motion Picture Studios (AAMPS). Audience Alliance is a consortium based out of California and Australia. Peter Rancie is the CEO and founder of this film company.

Once the contract was signed, Bonnie and I traveled several times to California for movie meetings. At our very first meeting, we met several individuals who would be instrumental in casting the movie. Because of the close ties Audience Alliance had with Australia, there was conversation about the possibility of having Russell Crowe play my part in the movie.

Now, how cool would that be!

You might not like his politics, but that boy can act. He is one of the most recognized actors in the world. For the next few weeks, I fantasized about being on the movie set with Russell Crowe. My fantasy, however, came crashing down when we learned that Russell gets paid $20,000,000 per film. Yikes!

So much for flying with that Crowe!

During the Q&A sessions, I often relate the above story about Russell Crowe playing me in the movie.

Then when pressed, "Mike, who is *really* going to play your part in the film?"

I tell the audience,

"After the casting people first met me and had spent some time with me, I was certain they would choose my look-alike—Brad Pitt. However, as the days passed, they unanimously agreed . . . Pee-wee Herman would be their man."

Hey, it works for me!

POPCORN IN THE PARK

- Where will the *Train to Potevka* movie premier be held?

There have been discussions that the movie premier will be held in three locations: Hollywood, New York City, and, also . . . Bear River City. Not having a theater in our little town, the plan would be to set up a large tent in the park, one that will hold at least 500 people. At one end of the tent will be a huge football stadium screen. Then, during the weekend of the premier, we will invite all the cowboys from northern Utah and southern Idaho, and everyplace in-between, to join us for opening night.

What a great idea, and what fun we will have!

SCREENPLAY BLUES

● Did you get to help with the screenplay?

As mentioned in another section of this book, one of the big struggles we are having moving the film forward, is the differences of opinion we have about the screenplay which, of course, is the basic outline for the movie. Several of us working on the film want to stay as close as possible to the *Potevka* book, which is in contrast to movie producers' demand to turn the film into a "007," "James Bond," "Jason Bourne" spy thriller, which *A Train to Potevka* is not. The following, unfinished story is to share with you some of the frustration of helping to write a screenplay.

I bid farewell to the old babushka, tied down the ear flaps of my Russian shapka, and hoisted my duffel bag over my shoulder.

As I walked out of the dilapidated train station into the storm, I noticed a large dog curled up under the station overhang which was providing the mutt little protection from the blowing, drifting snow. The skinny, frail dog raised his snow-covered head and looked up at me.

"Stay warm, boy. It's going to be a rough one tonight," I said, as I started off through the deep, heavy snow.

Having walked only a short distance in the direction of the safe house, I stopped to look behind me to see if I was being followed. No stranger, no Russian mafia, no KGB, but there, thirty feet behind me, jumping from one of my footprints to another, was the dog I had seen only minutes earlier at the train station.

"Boy, you've got to get home and back to your owner," I said. "You're going to get lost out here on a night like this."

After walking another hundred yards, I turned around and there he still was. Whenever I'd stop, he'd stop and stare in my direction. At one point, I set my gear and duffle down and walked back towards him. With each step I took towards him, he would step back, keeping the same distance between us; all the while, never taking his eyes off me.

When I stopped to rest from the difficult struggle I was having against the blowing, heavy snow, I used my best command to voice warn him,

"Get on home now! You have no idea what trouble you'd get yourself into hooking up with me." *As I lectured him, he lay in the snow looking directly at me but did not budge.*

Cold, hungry, and anxious to get to the safe house, I again grabbed my gear and plodded on through the storm.

Following only verbal instructions given me by headquarters, I walked about a mile before I came upon a cabin near the edge of the forest. As directed, I searched under the huge rock at the side of the izba until my fingers became numb from the cold. After finding the key, it took five minutes or more before I could get my frozen fingers and hands to cooperate in order to open the padlock. Once the door was open, I moved my gear inside. The mangy mutt sat twenty-five feet from the cabin watching my every move. One last time I tried to shoo him away in the direction of the station. I even tried throwing a snowball at him, not very effectively, however, considering how tired, famished, and frozen I was. I sensed his lack of concern when the snowball landed only halfway between us.

"Boy, get out of here. Go on!" I felt so sorry for the malnourished mongrel.

Once inside, my first priority was checking for KGB listening devices. Thankfully, there were none.

Feeling much better now that I was out of the elements, I went directly to the cupboards, pulled back the tarp that served as a door and . . . nothing. No MREs (Meals Ready to Eat)! I stood momentarily paralyzed. How could this possibly be? Believing that the safe house was equipped with seven days' worth of MREs was what had sustained me during my five days without food while riding the slow-moving, frozen train halfway across Russia.

Having seen the wardrobe up against the back wall when I entered the cabin, I opened the door, certain it contained the MRE provisions. Again nothing. In a panic, I began searching under the floor boards and the overhead rafters. Still nothing. I sat down on the edge of the bed, trying to convince myself that this wasn't real.

Having gone so long without food, I had been counting the days until I would get to the safe house and the MREs. After a thorough search, the only thing I found in the cabin was a bowl of old, rotten apples. So where were the MREs? Had someone been in the cabin? And why had *headquarters told me there were provisions here?*

Trying to put a positive spin on the situation, I tried to convince myself that in the morning I'd be able to buy the provisions I needed at the village market.

Too tired and weak to chop wood to make a fire, I placed my gear under the bed and took off my boots. I pulled the heavy table across the room with the intention to position it against the cabin door. I opened the door one last time to check the storm. Totally forgotten, there, curled up next to the stone steps under the cabin overhang, was the brown dog. He stood, shook off the snow, and looked at me, preparing to run if I approached him.

"Dang it, you stupid mutt. You'll freeze to death out here. Get out of here!"

He just stood watching me, blinking his eyes, as the heavy snow continued to fall.

I shut and locked the door, then pushed the big oak table against it.

Totally spent from all I had gone through since our covert mission was compromised, I fell, exhausted, onto the bed. I pulled the entire pile of six or seven blankets over me and wondered how many days I could sleep before my empty stomach rebelled and woke me up. After several minutes, my body heat began to warm my cocoon. It was the first time I'd been warm in days. Sleep, wonderful sleep! Yet, exhausted as I was, sleep wouldn't come. I lay there for what seemed a half hour or more.

"That dang dog!"

I threw back the blankets, stood and walked to the door. Angry for what I was doing, I pushed back the table. I slowly opened the door; there stood the brown dog.

This time he didn't back away.

"Okay, but only until morning when the storm breaks," I said. "Come on, get in here."

He just stood and looked at me.

I knelt down and slapped at my knee, "Come on, it's okay." He didn't budge.

Finally, I moved back away from the door. After shaking off the snow, ever so slowly the dog walked in and stood at the other side of the table near the cabin window. I slowly pushed the table up against the door and locked it. I crawled back in bed and bid my new roommate goodnight.

"Ok, Mr. Brown, I'll see you in the morning. Well, actually, as hammered as I am," I mumbled, "it will probably be sometime in the late afternoon that I'll see you."

When I blew out the candle on the small table next to the bed, he was still standing across the room near the window watching me.

When I woke in the morning, my new roommate was asleep curled up on the end of the bed.

"Good morning Mr. Brown," I said quietly through a yawn not wanting to startle him.

Slowly he lifted his head and looked at me, surely wondering what my reaction would be to his boldness of getting on the bed during the night.

"Mr. Brown, it's okay. Had I been in your skin and with a storm like that raging outside, I'd have done the same thing. So, can we assume that you don't have a home or someone to take care of you? But I'm here for only a few days and then you're on your own again, Mr. B."

He looked at me as if he understood.

I sat up in the bed and reached my hand down to pet him, but he pulled away.

Suddenly he leaped from the bed and dashed across the room. At the cabin window, he stood on his hind legs and *looked out as we heard the howling of wolves coming from the nearby forest. The louder the wolves became, the more agitated Mr. B. seemed. He started pacing, growling and whining; he would look over at me and then out the window towards the forest in the direction of the wolves.*

"It's all right Mr. B., they can't get in here; and with the two of us together, they won't dare mess with us."

As he looked out the window, I walked over to him and patted his head. He looked up at me, seeming to say, "Don't worry, it's okay, I'll take care of you by keeping the wolves away."

I turned and walked to the bed where I pulled on my boots. Mr. B jumped up on the bed and lay down next to me while the mournful wailing of the wolves continued. After approximately 10 minutes, the unsettling howling stopped.

"Mr. B., how about us chopping some wood to make a fire in the stove and warm this place up?"

I pulled on my cold weather gear, moved the table away from the door, and undid the lock. Cautiously, I stepped out into the storm onto the stone steps with Mr. B. at my side. No sign of the wolves. I pulled the door shut and we trudged through the snow to the woodpile next to the cabin. I pulled back the tarp and . . .

The previous story was my own creative attempt dealing with only a small segment of the film. If you've read *A Train to Potevka,* you will recognize the scene from the book, but here we chose to try the added dimension of a dog. Personally, I thought it created a strong element to the story. I was certain the creative director would like it. He did not, and it was rejected. So goes the frustration of working on my first movie screenplay.

And I thought I could write!

VIGNETTES AND THE SEQUEL

A BODY FALLING APART

- Why did it take so long to write your second book?

The movie company doing *A Train to Potevka* has run into several bumps along the way. The movie was originally targeted to be released last year. One thing I've learned; it definitely takes a long time to put together a major motion picture.

It was my intention to release the sequel to *Potevka* a few months after the film was distributed to movie theaters. However, with these bumps in the road and other complications contributing to the movie's delay, many people suggested that I write an interim book and release the sequel to *A Train to Potevka* at a later time.

Twenty-four months ago I started to write this book of vignettes. I planned that it would be primarily for those readers who had enjoyed *A Train to Potevka*.

No sooner had I begun to write this book, when I tore my knee while playing racquetball. Once the surgery was done and I began my physical therapy, the doctors discovered that I had a serious problem with the blood flow in my leg. Therefore, not long after my knee surgery, I went back into the hospital and had surgery on my leg to correct the blood supply problem. For several months thereafter, I was doing physical therapy not only to rehabilitate my knee, but also to regain the muscle strength I had lost in my leg.

I was very dedicated in doing my physical therapy because my goal was to be back playing on the racquetball court within six months. Almost four months to the day of my first surgery, I was allowed to start playing again. Within a few weeks I had my game back and was competing against my racquetball buddies five days a week, Monday through Friday, at Hill Air Force Base. Just like old times!

Months later I was playing against my greatest nemesis, Ryan Montgomery. Ryan is a handsome, physical specimen. He played on the Utah State racquetball team and is decades my junior. Because of my two previous surgeries, we had not played against one another for several months.

During a critical moment of the match, he was running full speed from the front wall towards the back. I was running full speed from the back wall towards the front. It was in the middle of the court that the "mother of all" collisions took place.

When I got up off the floor and came to my senses, I couldn't feel my right shoulder, and my arm was hanging down at my side. Being dumb and stupid, like many old jocks are, we went on and finished the game. (Ask Ryan who won.)

A few days later, Bonnie and I boarded a plane for Europe, where, for two weeks, I did lectures on a cruise ship while sailing through Scandinavia, the Baltics, and Russia. By the time we returned home to Utah, I could barely lift my right arm above my waist.

Despite my aversion to doctors and thinking it would eventually heal on its own, Bonnie dragged me to the hospital. After the X-rays we were told I had severely torn my rotator cuff; the doctors scheduled surgery for a month later.

When I came out of the anesthetic, the head orthopedic surgeon told me,

"Sir, the surgery was successful. In about a year, with dedicated physical therapy, you should regain at least 90% of the use of your arm."

"What about racquetball? Will I ever be able to play again?"

Rather than reply, the two surgeons, without saying a word, just rolled their eyes while shaking their heads from side to side. I assumed that meant . . . no.

I would not recommend rotator cuff surgery to anyone unless absolutely necessary. Besides all the complications, pain, and sickness that accompanied my surgery . . . what else could possibly go wrong?

Unbelievably, during my recovery time I came down with staph infection.

Within hours it had spread to my eyes, nose, and mouth. It spread so quickly, the doctors were unsure how they could control it. In fact, with the infection moving so fast, in the middle of the night a team of doctors came into my room and advised me that they were not sure they would be able to save me.

They kept me in the hospital in the Intensive Care Unit for several days with powerful antibiotics flowing from an IV in an attempt to kill the staph and keep me alive. It was a bit disconcerting to see every person who entered my room put on a protective suit before getting close to me, and then remove that covering and put it into the biohazard waste container before leaving my room.

Finally, I was able to return home, but spent weeks in a recliner, continuing to take heavy doses of strong antibiotics. For three months, I rarely left the house. The one-two punch of surgery and the staph infection left me so weak there were many times I thought I was not going to make it.

When I finally started to recover from the staph infection, I became very discouraged because of the constant pain in my shoulder and the frightening lack of mobility in my arm. It never crossed my mind to even think about playing racquetball or other sports again. To lose the camaraderie of playing with "the guys," and the physical health benefits of competitive sports was especially disheartening.

When going to the hospital for my follow ups, I would have the occasion to meet others who had gone through the same rotator cuff surgery. Most of them told me that the turning point would happen at about the twelve-month mark; I would start feeling better and begin regaining the mobility I had lost.

At the three-month point, I started doing physical therapy in earnest. Going to the clinic, to be abused by the therapist three times each week, was one of the most difficult things I have ever had to do. To lie on a table and have them push, pull, and stretch my frozen shoulder was, at times, almost more than I could bear.

Then at about the eighth or ninth month, I finally crossed that invisible barrier I had been told about—the therapy became easier, the pain lessened, and the thoughts of someday playing racquetball again started to dance in my mind.

At the twelve-month point of rehabilitation, I was given the green light to once again start playing racquetball. I'm happy to report that, yes, I am back on the court playing four or five days a week. However, I'm playing smarter, with a lot more caution, but I'm enjoying it more than I ever have.

So, when people ask why it has taken so long to write the second book, I ask them,

"How much time do you have?" so I can give them a blow-by-blow of my three racquetball surgeries accompanied by a strong dose of staph infection—all in a twenty-four month period.

I'm reminded of the statement my orthopedic surgeon said to me during my last visit as we were saying goodbyes,

"Mike, I think it's about time you started acting your age," he admonished me.

Now, if I could only follow his advice.

RUSSIA: RAGS AND RICHES . . . SPIES AND LIES

- When will the sequel to *A Train to Potevka* be released and what will it cover?

This is one of the most commonly asked questions that I get. The reason the sequel has not been released is because we felt it best not to make the sequel available until after the release of the film, which is based upon, of course, the first book. In spite of the on-going movie delays, the sequel is scheduled to be released next fall. Its title: *Russia: Rags and Riches—Spies and Lies*.

There are three main parts to the sequel: (1) Who brought my sister Karen's package to me in Potevka—and no, it was not the Three Nephites; (2) What happened to the young boy Sasha, who helped me and the two elders get into McDonald's; and (3) The last section of the sequel details how my career ended because of Robert Hanssen.

If you are interested, I suggest that you rent the DVD entitled *Breach*. Robert Hanssen was the senior FBI agent who worked as a mole inside our intelligence services. For a period of 17 years he provided classified, top secret information to the KGB and Soviet intelligence. It is said that Robert Hanssen did more damage to our U.S. national security than all other U.S. spies combined.

When it became evident that there was a mole within our intelligence community, our State Department went to great lengths to find him and stop the damage he was causing to our intelligence efforts.

In the beginning, the information he passed on to the Soviets was not all that damaging. As the years went by, however, and Hanssen leaked more and more sensitive information, our domestic and foreign policies were dealt a severe blow. When Russian agents working for us were murdered, the State Department determined to make a concentrated effort to find and capture the mole, once and for all.

Within our federal government we have 16 intelligence agencies. These include the CIA, FBI, DIA, NSA, etc. Each branch of the military—Army, Air Force, Navy, and

Marines—has their own intelligence services. In an effort to find the mole, two of the very best agents from each of the 16 intelligence services were sent to Washington, D.C. to be part of the task force mandated to finally catch the mole. And who did they choose to help head up this task force? Unbelievably . . . none other than the mole himself—Robert Hanssen.

Prior to his being discovered, U.S. intelligence focused on three suspects: Robert Hanssen, a naval intelligence officer, and myself.

After Robert Hansen had been captured, I learned that for several years Hanssen had used part of my code name. Because of his work as a senior Soviet analyst and my work in Russia and the former Soviet Union, Hanssen and I had several things in common. I never remember meeting him, but I hope to, someday. I want to look into the eyes of the man that caused Bonnie and me to go through a living hell of being investigated for treason by the FBI and CIA. Thus, my next book, *Russia: Rags and Riches—Spies and Lies,* will detail the experiences Bonnie and I went through during the 28 months I was a suspect.

THE PUBLISHING PARADOX

- Why did you choose to self publish?

When I wrote *A Train to Potevka*, it was never my intention to publish or market the book. After writing the ten-page original short story about receiving my sister Karen's package while at the safe house in *Potevka*, I received a lot of encouragement from Bonnie and our friends to write more of my stories. But, again, I never dreamed it would end up being an actual book.

Surprisingly, as the memories started coming back, I found that the more I wrote, the more it seemed I wanted to write. I found the best time to do this was between 11:00 PM and 2:00 AM when there was no phone ringing and the "honey do's" could be put off until the next day. I probably wrote two to three hours each evening, every second or third night.

Once the manuscript was finished, it was my intention to get a dozen copies printed to give away. However, we soon learned there were no printers willing to print a measly dozen copies. After a week or so of searching, Bonnie was able to find a printer in Tennessee willing to print their minimum run—100 copies.

Once we got the printed copies back, we gave the first 60 copies away to family and friends. Within the next few weeks, people started to call inquiring as to where the book could be purchased. Surprised by such phone calls, Bonnie and I started to consider that the book might actually have some marketability after all. Thus, we did an initial test market in Tremonton, Brigham City, and Logan.

Not having a publisher or local printer, we soon realized we were getting in way over our heads. We needed help! We studied the Yellow Pages as to possible publishers in the Intermountain area. We recognized only two or three names out of the dozens listed. For whatever reason, the name Essex Publishing stood out.

Why not give it a chance, I thought.

While doing our preliminary research, we learned that publishers want only printed manuscripts submitted, not the actual book. Therefore, it was a copy of our manuscript which we sent to Essex Publishing's offices in Salt Lake City.

A week had passed when we got a form letter from Essex telling us they had received the manuscript and would get back to us in the next four months.

"Four months?" I said to Bonnie. "Why should it take four months to read my manuscript? We're already getting emails and phone calls from people who want to buy copies of the book, even multiple copies."

One week later I received a phone call from an Essex executive telling me that four staff people had read *A Train to Potevka* and loved it. "Mike, our company wants to be your publisher!" she said.

After the phone call, I was so excited I ran downstairs to tell Bonnie. She was in the living room visiting with a neighbor. I was so happy, I hugged them both. The three of us immediately celebrated with a round of beers, the "root" kind of course.

Within the next few days, a contract from Essex arrived. However, after reading the contract in detail, I couldn't believe what the arrangement would be. I was going to give them all rights to the book, and they were going to keep most of the money. Not only that, they wanted the rights to any future books that I might write as part of this same arrangement.

There is something not quite right about this, I thought.

After reading the contract several times to ensure I understood its contents, I called Essex Publishing and told them of my concerns.

"You have to understand," they said, "you are a brand new author and the compensation package we're offering you is standard in the industry."

"But according to my calculations, Essex Publishing will pay me only 60¢ to 70¢ per book. I want to know, after all the expenses are taken out, who gets the $6.00 that is left over?" I questioned.

The executive on the other end of the line replied,

"Well, Essex Publishing, of course, gets the $6.00."

"And why in world, in the name of fairness, should Essex get $6.00 for each of my books when I did all the work to write it, and I will still be the one doing all the work to market it?"

Then the lady on the other end of the phone said to me,

"Mr. Ramsdell, the reason we get the $6.00 is because of our name, Essex Publishing."

At that moment I made one of the best decisions I would ever make.

"I appreciate your interest in my book," I said, "but I think I'll go in another direction. Have a nice day!"

How some things seem to work out is a total mystery.

It was only a few days later that I received the amazing call from Costco which eventually led to them ordering, over the next several weeks, 30,000 books; more than I could sell by myself in the next few years. From our personal savings, we were able to finance the first large printing. And the rest—as they say—is history.

From that exasperating experience with Essex Publishing, I promised myself that if *Potevka* became successful, I would do what I could to help other self-published authors. Yes, there are pros and cons on both sides of the publishing dilemma; to self publish or sell your soul to a big publisher? However, as I tell all would-be authors, why not try it yourself first? You maintain control, you are your own boss, and you make the decisions. Why not be the captain of your own ship?

So often I hear a story about a young author who signs on with a national or local publisher. The monetary rewards, in most cases, are meager for the author and only financially beneficial to the publishing company—unless, of course, you happen to be John Grisham or Tom Clancy.

Not long ago I was doing a book signing in Scottsdale, Arizona, when one afternoon a young lady came to my table, her shopping cart full of groceries. She was the first person I ever met while doing a Costco signing who also had a book of her own in Costco. Certainly, we had a lot to talk about.

When I asked her about the relationship she had with her New York publisher—specifically, how her contract had worked out—it was evident she did not want to talk about it. Later, when I told her of the advantages I had found by self publishing, she finally opened up.

During the last three years, she had made her New York publisher over three million dollars. In those same three years she had been compensated less than twenty thousand dollars. She obviously had not read the fine print in the contract. As we spoke, she became visibly emotional.

"I can't get out of the contract," she said. "And even worse, my contract stipulates that the publishing company has the rights to all future books."

This is a prime example as to why I plead with new authors to do their research and get all the information they can in order to make an informed decision about what will work best for them.

Whenever I have the opportunity to do a presentation, I usually mention my strong belief that there is a book in each one of us. The best books are about the human spirit rising above hardship. My book is certainly not great literature, however it is about life . . . my life.

"Yes," I tell the audience, "maybe you weren't a covert agent in Russia, but (trying to a add little humor) maybe you, too, had four older brothers who enjoyed kicking you around like a soccer ball."

Think of how many times we are urged to write our own personal histories. And think what a blessing that history or story will be to your family, your friends, and to your posterity. Yes, getting started can be intimidating, but the challenges of writing, editing, printing, marketing, and distributing your book can also be a great adventure. I respectfully encourage you to give it a try. Who knows, you might be on Oprah long before I ever will.

And to think how close I was to signing my soul over to Essex Publishing when, as a self-published author, we estimate over a million-plus people have now read *A Train to Potevka.*

As the Nike ad says . . . Just do it!

QUESTIONS
A MIXED BAG

POTEVKA'S PLACE

• Is the village of Potevka a real place?

It comes as a disappointment to many readers that *Potevka* is a fictionalized name. However, when you stop to think about it, can you imagine how tall the tree would be that

U.S. Intelligence would hang me from if I were to reveal the actual name of the village in the middle of Russia where U.S. Intelligence has a safe house. It really is a no-brainer.

You can't imagine the letters and emails I've received concerning the location of *Potevka*. Readers write to me about the lengths they have gone to in trying to locate the village, including using resources such as Google Earth, NASA, National Geographic, etc.

People, also, question me about the correct pronunciation of *Potevka*. I chose the name because of how the word rolls so easily off the tongue. The name is very easy to pronounce when one knows that it originated from my very favorite musical, *Fiddler on the Roof*. Remember the name of the Russian village from the movie—*Anatevka*—and the beautiful song of the same name? The village of Potevka is named in honor of the poor people of Russia—like *Anatevka*—thus the name *Po-tevka*.

A HOLEY HEAD

• Can we see the holes in your head?

Strange as it may sound, I am surprised at how many people ask if they can see the holes in my head. This question, of course, relates to

247

an incident I write about in *A Train to Potevka* when I was caught by the KGB and the Russian mafia. The beating I suffered was done with a pair of brass knuckles which left a number of holes in my head. Thus the question:

"Can we see the holes in your head?"

And my reply, "Yes, you can, depending on the number of rubles you have in your wallet."

ROLLING THE MUS BUS

• Do you still have your Volkswagen van—the Mus Bus?

Yes, I still have my Mus Bus. It turned 40 years old this year.

A few years ago, when the movie people discussed the possibility of using the Mus Bus in the film, I took it to Maaco for a new paint job and then to a VW mechanic for a serious overhaul. With a new rebuilt engine and new paint, the Mus Bus looked like and performed as if it had just come off the showroom floor.

During the summer, as often as we could, Bonnie and I have enjoyed using it to visit our favorite canyon destinations. Midsummer, we drove the Mus Bus up to Midway, Utah, for an impromptu family gathering. Once the party was over and we were ready to drive home, the Mus Bus, for whatever reason, would not start.

We pushed it, jumped it, and tried everything possible, but it refused to even sputter.

Finally, we called our insurance company, USAA, and arranged to have it towed to a repair shop in Heber. We were able to catch a ride home with another couple who also lived near us in Davis County.

The following morning, just before church, I received a telephone call from the tow truck driver telling me,

"Mr. Ramsdell, I'm sorry but I have some bad news. It seems the tie-down cables failed and your Mus Bus came off the tow truck, crashed through a farmer's fence, rolled down a field, and ended up in a ditch."

Needless to say, after owning my Mus Bus for all those 38 years, I sadly realized that our fun times together were now over. I was not a happy camper. Nor was the Mus Bus.

However, thankfully, all was not lost. After negotiating with the tow truck's insurance company, they gave me two options: get a large, lump sum payment—I didn't know that the Mus Bus, 40 years old, is now considered a classic and worth 10 times more than what it originally cost—or have the Mus Bus totally repaired. We chose the second option.

Recently Bonnie and I paid a visit to Ken Garff's Collision Repair in Clearfield. After four months, they tell me they are almost through with the needed repairs and restoration. I'm hoping to get my Mus Bus back at least by next spring, when you will find Bonnie and me driving the highways and byways of the beautiful canyons of the Rocky Mountains.

And also, the Mus Bus gets its own cameo in the movie.

WHERE ARE THEY NOW?

During the question-and-answer period, I am often asked about the main characters in my book: where are they now?

My son, Chris:

Chris finished his studies at the University of Utah and then graduated from dental school at the University of Maryland. His dental practice is in Centerville, Utah

Chris and his wife, Jen, are the proud parents of three beautiful daughters: Ellen, Phebe, and Hazel. I love my granddaughters: they are dancers, soccer players, gymnasts, and budding musicians. However, they have little interest in throwing a football or trying to hit a backhand on the tennis court.

Then, two years ago, the "event" finally happened when Jen gave birth to my little grandson, Isaac, AKA "Jimmer." Since he was six months old, whenever he sees his Papa, all he wants to do is throw a ball with me. I can definitely see him in his early twenties as the starting quarterback for the Utes or Cougars. But, hopefully, it will be for my Aggies.

Brigham Redd:

Brigham Redd is the elder I wrote about in *A Train to Potevka* who, along with Elder Pitts, was with me the night we went to the McDonald's at Pushkin Square in Moscow and met the Russian, orphan boy, Sasha. After his mission, Brigham Redd went on to graduate from Ohio State University Medical School and became an orthopedic surgeon. He now works in private practice in Idaho Falls, Idaho.

Sasha:

The story as to what happened to the orphan boy, Sasha, will be detailed in the sequel, *Russia: Rags and Riches—Spies and Lies,* scheduled to be released next fall.

Koshka:

Vladimir Koshka, the mafia boss who was instrumental, along with the KGB, in compromising the American Embassy in Moscow, continued his mafia work throughout Russia. Interpol and U.S. Intelligence waited patiently for Koshka and his men to make their next ill-advised move, which they eventually did. What happened to Koshka will, also, be part of the sequel.

Yuri Novotny's Family:

As to the family of Yuri Novotny, a U.S. Air Force Captain whom I befriended while teaching at the intelligence school in Oberammergau, Germany, please see *A Babushka's Scolding* in Chapter 12, *Keynotes and Firesides*.

My Brothers:

My brothers all live in Utah: Dee in Bear River, Ted in Salt Lake City, and Dick in Garland. Our half brother, Jack, who lived in Carson City, Nevada, passed away a few years ago. My brothers are all retired and slowing down because of the health problems associated with age. Yet, the three of them still get together at least once a month at a local Chinese buffet only a few miles from where I live to commiserate and relive the good times of their youth.

My Sisters:

My sister, Sally, still lives with her husband Boyd in Garland, Utah where she tries to keep track of 18 grandchildren and 23 great grandchildren. Yikes!

My sister, Karen "Pickle" Loo, still lives in Torrance, California, and divides her time spoiling grandkids in San Diego and Sandy, Utah.

GETTING PERSONAL

FAVORITES

I am often asked, especially during the Q&A sessions, several personal questions, usually the same ones over and over. With apologies to those who couldn't care less about my personal preferences, my likes and dislikes, I have included in this section my responses to the most frequently asked personal questions. If this has no interest for you, please skip this portion of the book.

Food:

Being a Ramsdell, I like it all: American, Asian, Italian, Mexican, etc. Because of my many years living in Germany, I also have a strong affinity for German food—the more vinegar, the better.

Place to Eat:

There are many—the Mandarin (Bountiful), Corbin's (Layton), Maddox (Brigham City)—

but if I had to choose, I would say prime rib and crab legs at the Rio Resort in Las Vegas, Nevada. When doing book signings every few months in Nevada, if Bonnie and I don't eat there at least once during our visit . . . we get the shakes.

Music:

During my teenage years folk music became extremely popular across America, and I love that genre of music: The Kingston Trio, John Denver, The Brothers Four. As for contemporary music, I am a big fan of Sting and Paul Simon. Also, there are few artists equal to the talent of Andrea Bocelli. However, as to my very favorite music, one of my greatest joys is to be on our deck, looking out over the lake on an early summer evening with Bonnie and our cats, listening to the beautiful music of Wolfgang Amadeus Mozart. In my opinion, he is the greatest composer that ever lived. I am of the belief that such classical music surely comes from Him above.

Books:

There are so many, it would be hard to choose just one. Some of my favorites: *War and Peace, Grapes of Wrath, Brothers Karamozov, Les Miserable, Great Expectations, Doctor Zhivago, Red Badge of*

Courage, Huckleberry Finn, Anna Karenina, and *A Farewell to Arms.*

As for contemporary work, one of the best I have read in the last several years is a book written by David Baldacci entitled *Wish You Well.* If you haven't read it, please do. As a storyteller, there are few better than Baldacci. I wish I had a small kernel of the writing talent that this man has.

Movies:
    1) *Empire of the Sun,*
    2) *The Pianist,* and
    3) *Saving Private Ryan.*

All three of these powerful films are based on actual events that, during a time of war, depict the worst of humanity and, yet, the eventual triumph of the human spirit. As such, in my opinion, they ought to be mandatory viewing and study for every high school student.

Actor:
There is so much young talent in the movie industry today, however, I think the best actors are those who continue to prove themselves through the years: Morgan Freeman, Judi Dench, Geoffory Rush, and Cate Blanchett to name just a few.

Sports:

I love sports, but my passions are racquetball, tennis, and skiing. A lifelong tennis player, my sport of choice now is racquetball.

Although getting along in years, I'm still competitive, play as often as possible—four to five times a week—and I feel I can still keep up with the best of them.

There are few things more enjoyable for me than to go to the gym at Hill Air Force Base and be challenged by a young airman to a match. I'm certain that when he first meets me he is thinking, *This old guy is dead meat.* In most cases, however, when the match is over, the young airman leaves the court with his tail between his legs, thinking . . . *how can that old goat run me ragged like that?*

I do love playing racquetball!

As to a favorite spectator sport, football comes first. I've become a big fan of Boise State, the perennial David-kicking-Goliath around every weekend. Also, having played football my freshman year at Utah State, I still love and support my Aggies.

In addition, I am a big fan of professional tennis, especially the major championships: the Australian Open, the French Open, Wimbledon, and our own U.S. Championship. Bonnie and I have had the good fortune to be spectators at three of these major events.

Places to Visit:

During my career, I have been blessed to visit many countries around the world. I've lived in Europe, Scandinavia, and Russia for a dozen years or more. While living in these various countries, Bonnie and I have taken the opportunity to travel and experience many other cultures.

Once retired, I thought our days of international travel were over. However, for the last four years, I have been fortunate to be asked to do lectures on various cruise ships— Norwegian, Royal Caribbean, Princess, Costa, and Carnival. Never having cruised before, we found we really enjoyed the lifestyle: the excitement of being at sea, the ports of call, the entertainment, the food, and especially, the opportunity to make friends with so many wonderful people from around the world.

When I was first assigned to Scandinavia, I was taken aback by its beauty and the fact there is water everywhere. I would love someday to rent a small cabin at a seaside village in Norway, Sweden, or Finland and spend my summers writing by the water.

As for my favorite foreign city, I have to say Stockholm, Sweden. I have found during my years of travel and living abroad that Americans usually vacation in Europe by visiting the capitals of Paris, Berlin, Rome, London, Vienna, Madrid, etc. Therefore, when talking to fellow travelers, I always recommend that they remember to one day visit the beautiful countries of Scandinavia. There is no place like it.

My favorite place to visit in the United States is the New England area: Massachusetts, Connecticut, New Hampshire, Vermont, Rhode Island, and Maine—especially in the fall. Visiting these states during autumn is nothing less than spectacular. For those who have not been to New England during late September or early October, I highly recommend such a trip be added to your bucket list.

Historical Figure:

When asked if I could go back in time and meet with one of the great historical figures, who would it be? My answer is always Abraham Lincoln. It was while doing a political science paper as a student at Utah State that I became fascinated with this great man. It is amazing that despite his upbringing, disappointments, defeats, and all the challenges he suffered during the years of the Civil War, he left such a great, lasting legacy while holding our nation together.

GREATEST INFLUENCE

- Who had had the greatest influence in your life?

There are many. Regrettably, because my dad was quite old when I was a boy and had already raised a large family, he and I were never that close. I think he had spent all his energies raising my older brothers and sisters. However, he was very close to my four older brothers, and I always envied the relationship they had with our dad.

Unfortunately, because of the age difference between me and my older brothers, an average of twelve years, I was never able to develop the strong relationship with them that brothers should have. They were born almost one year after another, and, for whatever reason, they never let me inside their circle. Then, by the time I reached my teenage years, they had all left home, were married, and had started their own families and careers. Not having a close relationship with my brothers has always been one of my lasting regrets.

On the other hand, however, I have been greatly blessed throughout my life and career with an exceptional group of friends. Most of them are fellow officers with whom I served during my years in the military and in intelligence. Not only are they all patriots, having served our country honorably, but each has succeeded in their post-military careers and raised wonderful families. Though not blood brothers, these men are truly my *Brothers in Arms.*

Friend of my bosom, thou more than a brother, Why wert thou not born in my father's dwelling?

Charles Lamb

When it comes to the specific individual who has had the greatest influence on my life— it is my wife, Bonnie. As I write in the acknowledgement section of this book, after we were married, she joined me during the lean and mean of Russia and has been at my side ever since. She is dedicated, loyal, and loves me unconditionally. Because of her steadfast belief in me, she has helped me look beyond my self-imposed limitations and see the possibilities for a rich, fulfilling life while trying to lift and serve others at the same time.

When that day comes that I'm ready to leave this life and I look back, I'll know that whatever good I've been able to accomplish . . . I owe to my Bonnie.

THE BUCKET LIST?

- What is on your bucket list?

I really like this question. Besides, of course, wanting to be a good husband, father, papa, and friend, there are so many things with Bonnie I still want to do, places I want to visit, and experiences I want to have.

(1) Naturally, I hope to maintain my health through sensible diet and exercise.

(2) I want to continue playing competitive racquetball into my senior years.

(3) I want to see *A Train to Potevka* made into a successful major motion picture, provided it stays close to the book.

(4) I want to have the *Potevka* sequel, *Russia: Rags and Riches—Spies and Lies*, ready for release next fall.

(5) Once the movie is done and my book signings have slowed, I want to join a folk group that can use an extra voice and a few licks from my guitar and banjo. A few years ago, after returning home from Russia, I sang with a folk group that did mini-concerts at retirement communities. What a joy it was to bring a little music and happiness into their lives. I would love to do that again on a regular basis.

(6) I have been fortunate to be able to visit over 60 countries around the world and 48 of our United States. Someday, I want to visit Alaska and North Dakota to complete the domestic list.

(7) A big fan of college football, I would like to someday attend the Rose Bowl on New Year's Day in Pasadena, California. Hopefully, an undefeated Utah team—maybe even the Aggies—will be playing a top-ten team for the national championship of college football. Hey, I can dream, can't I?

(8) Inasmuch as tennis is one of the sports I love, I have played it most of my adult life. Having attended three of the four major championships—Wimbledon, the French Open, and the U.S. Open—I want to complete the list and one day travel Down Under to see the Australian Open.

(9) With Bonnie, I want to continue to live my life to the fullest, be the best person that I can, and, through my speaking and writing, lift others and help to remind us all of the importance of patriotism and how blessed we are to live in America.

Chapter 14

EPILOGUE

Nothing is worth more than this day.

Whatever you can do, or dream you can, begin it.   Boldness has genius, power, and magic in it.

Johann Wolfgang von Goethe

In the epilogue at the end of *A Train to Potevka*, I wrote the following:

And, yes, I do believe in angels. As a young boy, growing up in that wonderful, small town of Bear River, I had the blessing of being a little brother to one (Karen).   Then, many years later, another (Bonnie) came into my life . . . to heal my heart, teach me to love again, and bring peace and joy to this marvelous journey we are now traveling together called Life.

Little did I know when I wrote those words years ago, what an incredible journey this would be. Some mornings I have to pinch myself to realize this is not a dream: a best-selling book, one million-plus readers, hundreds of speaking events around the country, cruise ship lectures, a movie in the works, and my new book, *Potevka's Gifts,* just released.

And how has this all happened?

When I finished my work in Russia and was finally retired, Bonnie and I thought our future was all mapped out. After returning to the States, we would build our dream home, have time to travel and visit the parts of America we had not seen, take classes together at the university, spend our summers at the beach and on the tennis courts, and our winters on the ski slopes and the racquetball courts . . . basically enjoy the good life of retirement.

But the good Lord seemed to have a different plan, which He put in motion when I fractured my neck playing racquetball only a few weeks after we returned home from Russia.

As we are taught, blessings can come through adversity. In my case, I think back on the weeks after my accident—how angry, disappointed, and frustrated I felt. I was not someone you wanted to be around.

Then my life, my goals, and my future all changed when Bonnie suggested that I use my recovery time to write a short story for my grandkids about my time in Russia.

Yes, Bonnie and I did build our dream home close to the beautiful Rocky Mountains, and we do have the opportunity to see the major cities of America as we travel the country doing speaking events. However, taking classes at the university and the days we planned to be on the ski slopes and tennis courts still happen but very infrequently. However, we wouldn't have it any other way. I can't imagine a more rewarding retirement than what we have been blessed with.

I often think back on my years as an counterintelligence agent and, because of my work, never being able to share my feelings and love of country with others, which, at the time, I always regretted. The Lord made me wait for 30 years, but I now have the opportunity to share my thoughts, feelings, and experiences at hundreds of speaking events. Bonnie and I both feel strongly that this is our mission; what we are supposed to be doing at this time in our lives.

I strongly believe we are all on this journey of life together, and we are not here to fail. We have all been given gifts and talents to better our lives and the lives of those around us. It's never too late to make a difference. It's never too late to be someone's hero.

"Life gives to all a choice. You can satisfy yourself with mediocrity if you wish. You can be common, ordinary, dull, colorless . . .or you can channel your life so that it will be vibrant, progressive, useful, colorful, and rich."

Spencer W. Kimball

ACKNOWLEDGEMENTS

Thanks to my sister, Karen, who got this "Train" started by sending me a simple care package years ago to Russia. And I'm especially grateful to those who encouraged me to write about it . . . *A Train to Potevka.* Five years and a million-plus readers later, like us Bear River kids used to say . . . "Who would'a thunk it?"

A special thanks to my sister, Sally. After the book was published, her home in Garland became the number one place to buy books in Bear River Valley.

Thank you to the dozens of Costco managers around the West who were the first to believe in the book and were so supportive in its success.

Thanks to my distributor, Barry Reeder for all the help and support.

Also, thank you to all those who continue to work behind the scenes to get our *Potevka* movie made.

And finally, my greatest "Thank you" to my wife, Bonnie, who lived with me in Russia during the lean and hard times and has been at my side ever since. Bon, your belief in me is what has made it all happen. I will forever be grateful for the love, joy, and inspiration you bring into my life.

The Cossack and his Czarina

ABOUT THE AUTHOR

Mike was born and raised in Bear River, Utah. Upon graduation from Utah State University, he was commissioned an officer in the Military Intelligence Corp. After post-graduate studies at the University of Utah, he began his military active duty as a graduate from the Defense Language Institute (Russian and German) in Washington, D.C.

Lt. Colonel Ramsdell's career in Russian-Soviet counterintelligence has taken him on missions throughout Europe, Russia, Scandinavia, and Asia. Mike has served with U.S. and NATO Forces, various intelligence agencies, and the U.S. Department of State. His last foreign assignment was for a six-year period in Moscow and Gorky, Russia.

Mike currently lives in northern Utah with his wife, Bonnie, and their three cats: Gorbachev, Yeltsin, and Putin. A passion for racquetball, skiing, and college football, Mike also serves in the Sunday school of his local church. His best seller, *A Train to Potevka,* was Mike's first book, which was followed up by *Potevka's Gifts.* Next fall, his sequel, *Russia: Rags and Riches—Spies and Lies*, is scheduled for release.